Another 75 scenes from popular films to spark discussion

Videos That Teach 2

Another 75 scenes from popular films to spark discussion

Videos That Teach 2

DOUG FIELDS & EDDIE JAMES

Youth Specialties

ZONDERVAN™

GRAND RAPIDS, MICHIGAN 49530

Videos That Teach 2: Another 75 Scenes from Popular Films to Spark Discussion

Copyright © 2002 by Doug Fields and Eddie James

Youth Specialties Books, 300 S. Pierce St., El Cajon, CA 92020, are published by Zondervan Publishing House, 5300 Patterson Ave. S.E., Grand Rapids, MI 49530.

Published in association with the literary agency of Alive Communications, Inc., 7680 Goddard St., Suite 200, Colorado Springs, CO 80920.

Library of Congress Cataloging-in-Publication Data

Fields, Doug, 1962-
    Videos that teach 2 : another 75 scenes from popular films to spark discussion / Doug Fields and Eddie James.
      p. cm.
    Includes index.
    ISBN 0-310-23818-8
      1. Motion pictures in Christian education. 2. Christian eduction of teenagers.
I. Title: Videos that teach two. II. James, Eddie. III. Title.

BV1535.4 .F55 2002
268'.67—dc21

                                         2001039099

Unless otherwise indicated, all Scripture quotations are taken from the *Holy Bible: New International Version* (North American Edition). Copyright © 1973, 1978, 1984 by International Bible Society. Used by permission of Zondervan Publishing House.

Web site addresses listed in this book are current at the time of publication. Please contact Youth Specialties by e-mail (YS@YouthSpecialties.com) or by postal mail (Youth Specialties, Product Department, 300 South Pierce Street, El Cajon, CA 92020) to report URLs that are not operational and to suggest alternate URLs if available.

Edited by Laura Gross and Vicki Newby
Illustrations by Kyle White
Cover and interior design by DesignPoint, Inc.

Printed in the United States of America

03 04 05 06 07 08 / / 10 9 8

To Ted Lowe

Our lives are both better because of our friendship with you.
We sure love you!

Contents

The movies (in alphabetical order)

Acknowledgments

Thanks to Stephanie James, Cathy Fields, Ronny Higgins,
Tommy Woodard, Greg Early, Linda Kaye, Neely McQueen,
Bob Johns, Jeremy Webb, Gregg Farah, Gordon Wohlers,
David Smith, and Jeff Maguire for all your help, ideas, and friendship.
It's so great to have friends like you in our lives.

Quick Clip Locator BY TOPIC

Abandonment The Cider House Rules
Acceptance Gladiator
Accountability The Perfect Storm
Addiction 28 Days, Outbreak
Adoption The Cider House Rules
Adulthood My Dog Skip, October Sky
Adversity The Perfect Storm
Affection Mystery, Alaska
Afterlife Ghost
Ambition Gladiator
Anger Black Sheep, Star Wars: The Phantom Menace
Authenticity Angus
Bearing one another's burdens Brokedown Palace
Beauty The Saint
Being a light The Hurricane
Being lost Holy Man
Bitterness Big Daddy, One True Thing
Blessings Stepmom
Calamity Arlington Road
Cancer Stepmom
Caring Holy Man, Notting Hill
Challenges 28 Days; Girl, Interrupted; Keeping the Faith; The Natural;
 Notting Hill; The Perfect Storm; The Story of Us
Change Jurassic Park
Character Gladiator, The Saint
Cheating I.Q.
Child of God The Cider House Rules
Choices Erin Brockovich; Forces of Nature; Girl, Interrupted; Keeping the
 Faith; Pleasantville; Schindler's List
Circumstances Black Sheep, Meet Joe Black
Comfort Mr. Mom, Notting Hill
Commitment Chariots of Fire, Erin Brockovich, Runaway Bride, The Story
 of Us
Communication Frequency
Compassion Patch Adams, What about Bob?
Competitiveness The Cable Guy
Compliments As Good as It Gets
Compromise Jakob the Liar, Pleasantville
Confession Courage under Fire, Galaxy Quest
Conflict Black Sheep
Conscience Jakob the Liar
Consequences Where the Heart Is
Contentment One True Thing, A Simple Plan
Control Arlington Road, Big Daddy, Instinct, The Matrix
Convictions Chariots of Fire, Independence Day, The Patriot, Simon Birch
Courage Forever Young, Forrest Gump, Schindler's List
Dating Boys and Girls, Forever Young, Mission: Impossible 2
Death Stepmom
Deception Dirty Rotten Scoundrels, Galaxy Quest, I.Q., Jakob the
 Liar, The Messenger: The Story of Joan of Arc, Where the Heart Is
Decision making Girl, Interrupted; U-571
Defeat Mulan

Desires A Simple Plan
Destiny Simon Birch
Determination Mr. Smith Goes to Washington, The Perfect Storm
Differences Anywhere but Here, Austin Powers: International Man of
    Mystery, Ever After, Notting Hill
Diligence Mr. Smith Goes to Washington
Divorce For Love of the Game, The Story of Us
Dominion Instinct
Doubt Jurassic Park
Dreams October Sky, Patch Adams
Embarrassment Black Sheep
Encouragement As Good as It Gets; Mystery, Alaska
Ends justify the means I.Q.
Endurance The Natural
Eternity Ghost
Evangelism Forrest Gump, The Sixth Sense
Evil Arlington Road
Excuses The Prince of Egypt
Expectations The Breakfast Club, The Story of Us
Experience versus inexperience Forever Young, My Dog Skip
Facing your demons 28 Days, Courage under Fire
Failure Mulan
Faith The Green Mile
Faithfulness Forces of Nature, Runaway Bride
Fame EDtv
Family Erin Brockovich
Fear First Knight, Jurassic Park, Meet Joe Black, Mr. Mom, Pleasantville, Star
    Wars: The Phantom Menace, Where the Heart Is
Feelings Meet Joe Black, Pleasantville
Forgiveness Courage under Fire, Ever After, Jurassic Park, The Story of Us
Freedom Big Daddy, Independence Day
Friendship Brokedown Palace, The Cable Guy, First Knight, Forrest Gump,
    The Hurricane, My Dog Skip
Fruit of the Spirit Black Sheep
Generational sin Big Daddy, The Breakfast Club
God Frequency
God's calling Keeping the Faith, The Prince of Egypt
God's sovereignty The Prince of Egypt
God's will Keeping the Faith, Simon Birch
Good versus evil The Messenger: The Story of Joan of Arc, Star Wars: The
    Phantom Menace
Grace Brokedown Palace
Greed Toy Story 2
Growing up Anywhere but Here
Guilt Courage under Fire
Happiness A Simple Plan
Hate Star Wars: The Phantom Menace
Heaven and hell Forrest Gump, Ghost
Heroes October Sky, Schindler's List
High school Angus, Never Been Kissed
Holocaust Schindler's List
Honesty Austin Powers: International Man of Mystery, Big Momma's House,
    Courage under Fire, Forces of Nature, Forever Young, Meet Joe Black,
    While You Were Sleeping
Honor Anywhere but Here, Forrest Gump

Hope As Good as It Gets, The Hurricane, Jakob the Liar
Idols Mr. Mom, The Mummy
Inheritance Gladiator
Integrity Brokedown Palace, Chariots of Fire, Galaxy Quest, The
    Green Mile, I.Q.

Intimacy The Saint
Joy First Knight, One True Thing
Judging Big Momma's House
Judgment Day The Green Mile
Laughter Patch Adams
Leadership The Prince of Egypt, U-571
Legacy Gladiator
Life One True Thing
Life after death The Sixth Sense
Life lessons My Dog Skip
Listening Notting Hill
Living water Outbreak
Loneliness While You Were Sleeping
Loss Stepmom
Lost causes Mr. Smith Goes to Washington
Love Forces of Nature; Forever Young; For Love of the Game; Mystery, Alaska
Love of life Patch Adams
Loving ourselves Big Momma's House
Loving the unlovable The Cable Guy, What about Bob?
Loyalty Brokedown Palace, My Dog Skip
Lust Mission: Impossible 2
Making a difference Holy Man, Instinct
Marriage Forces of Nature; For Love of the Game; Mystery, Alaska; One True Thing; The Story of Us
Materialism A Simple Plan, Toy Story 2
Meanness The Cable Guy
Memories Frequency
Mercy What about Bob?
Miracles The Green Mile
Mistakes Jurassic Park, Never Been Kissed
Motives Jakob the Liar
New creation Pleasantville
Obsession The Cable Guy
Occult The Mummy
Opportunities The Natural
Pain The Breakfast Club, Dirty Rotten Scoundrels, Ever After, The Green Mile
Parent-child relationships Anywhere but Here, Austin Powers: International Man of Mystery, Big Daddy, For Love of the Game, Gladiator, October Sky, Stepmom
Parents The Breakfast Club, For Love of the Game
Passion Keeping the Faith
Patience Mr. Smith Goes to Washington
Peer pressure Angus, The Matrix, Never Been Kissed, Outbreak
Perseverance Mr. Smith Goes to Washington, The Natural, The Perfect Storm
Physical attraction Mission: Impossible 2
Playing God Instinct
Popularity Angus, Never Been Kissed
Power of words As Good as It Gets
Prayer Frequency, While You Were Sleeping
Pride Ever After
Priorities Erin Brockovich, Schindler's List
Privacy EDtv
Prophets The Messenger: The Story of Joan of Arc
Purity Boys and Girls
Purpose Gladiator, Keeping the Faith, Simon Birch
Questions Girl, Interrupted

Reality   28 Days, Galaxy Quest
Relationships   Boys and Girls, The Breakfast Club, EDtv, Frequency, Holy
   Man, The Sixth Sense
Reliability   Runaway Bride
Respect   My Dog Skip
Ridicule   Never Been Kissed
Risk   Forces of Nature, Holy Man
Role models   Forever Young
Running from the past   The Saint
Sabbath, the   Chariots of Fire
Sacrifice   Chariots of Fire
Safety   Arlington Road
Salvation   The Iron Giant, The Matrix, The Sixth Sense
Satan   The Messenger: The Story of Joan of Arc, The Mummy
Saying goodbye   Anywhere but Here
Secrets   Dirty Rotten Scoundrels
Security   Mr. Mom
Self-control   As Good as It Gets
Self-esteem   Angus
Self-sacrifice   The Iron Giant, Mr. Smith Goes to Washington
Selling your soul   EDtv
Service   First Knight, Patch Adams, What about Bob?
Sex   Boys and Girls
Sexuality   Mission: Impossible 2
Shame   Courage under Fire, Galaxy Quest
Significance   Instinct, The Patriot
Sin   Outbreak
Single parenting   Erin Brockovich
Spiritual warfare   Ghost, Independence Day
Stealing   Toy Story 2
Stereotypes   The Breakfast Club
Stress   Black Sheep
Substance abuse   28 Days
Suffering   Star Wars: The Phantom Menace
Taking a stand   The Patriot
Teamwork   Independence Day
Temptation   The Mummy, Toy Story 2
Ten Commandments   Toy Story 2
Terrorism   Arlington Road
Transparency   Meet Joe Black; Mulan; Mystery, Alaska; Notting Hill;
   Pleasantville
Trust   Ever After, Forces of Nature, Mr. Mom
Trusting God   The Cider House Rules
Truth   Ever After, Jakob the Liar, The Matrix, The Messenger: The Story of
   Joan of Arc
Unconditional love   Anywhere but Here
Understanding   Big Momma's House
Unity   The Hurricane, Independence Day, My Dog Skip
Values   Boys and Girls, Erin Brockovich, Schindler's List
Virginity   Boys and Girls
Virtues   Gladiator
Voyeurism   EDtv
Vulnerability   As Good as It Gets, Austin Powers: International Man of
   Mystery, Forever Young

Waiting   While You Were Sleeping
Wisdom   Big Momma's House, Jakob the Liar
Work   Erin Brockovich

Quick Clip Locator BY BIBLE REFERENCE

Genesis
17:5-8, 15-16xcThe Saint
32:28-30 . . . . The Saint
49:1-50:14 . . . . Stepmom

Exodus
3-4:23, 29-31 . . . . The Prince of Egypt
4:10-13 . . . . Meet Joe Black
20:8-11 . . . . Chariots of Fire
20:1-17 . . . . Toy Story 2

Leviticus
19:1-2, 11 . . . . I.Q.
26:40-42 . . . . Big Daddy

Deuteronomy
4:29-31 . . . . The Cider House Rules
5:6-22 . . . . Toy Story 2
18:17-22 . . .The Messenger: The Story of Joan
of Arc
23:21-23 . . . . Forces of Nature

Joshua
1:6-9 . . . . U-571

Ruth
1-4 . . . . While You Were Sleeping

1 Samuel
12:24-25 . . . Star Wars: The Phantom Menace
18:1-4 . . . . Forrest Gump
20:41-42 . . . . Forrest Gump

2 Samuel
22:29-37 . . . . The Hurricane

1 Kings
8:22-26, 54-60 . . . . Frequency
15:3 . . . . Big Daddy, The Breakfast Club

1 Chronicles
29:17 . . . . Jakob the Liar

2 Chronicles
1:7-12 . . . . U-571
20:9 . . . . Jurassic Park

Job
1:6-12 . . . . . .The Messenger: The Story of Joan
of Arc
1:8-2:10 . . . . The Natural
9 . . . . The Green Mile
22:2-3 . . . . The Patriot
36:15 . . . . The Perfect Storm
42:1-6, 12-17 . . . . The Natural

Psalm
5:1-3 . . . . Frequency
15:1-2 . . . . Meet Joe Black
22:27-28 . . . . Instinct
23 . . . . Mr. Mom
26:2-3 . . . . Jakob the Liar
27:10 . . . . Anywhere but Here
32:1-5 . . . . Courage under Fire
34 . . . . Star Wars: The Phantom Menace
34:4 . . . . Mr. Mom
34:11-14 . . . . Galaxy Quest
34:17-18 . . . . Mulan
37:4-9, 23-24 . . . . October Sky
40:1-5, 11-17 . . . . The Perfect Storm
49:16-20 . . . . EDtv
55:22 . . . . Courage under Fire
68:4-6 . . . . The Cider House Rules, While You
Were Sleeping
86:11 . . . . Boys and Girls
90 . . . . Star Wars: The Phantom Menace
91:9-12 . . . . Independence Day
103:15-16 . . . . EDtv
103:8-14 . . . . Jurassic Park
111:10 . . . . . Star Wars: The Phantom Menace
119:9-16 . . . . My Dog Skip, The Patriot
126 . . . . Patch Adams
139 . . . . The Saint, A Simple Plan
139:7-12 . . . . EDtv
139:13-16 . . . . Ever After

Proverbs
3:3 . . . . Brokedown Palace
3:21-26 . . . . Mulan
5:18 . . . . Forces of Nature
5:21-23 . . . . EDtv

Galatians

Ephesians

Philippians

Colossians

1 Thessalonians

2 Thessalonians

1 Timothy

2 Timothy

Titus

Hebrews

James

Eddie and I are thrilled that we've been asked to put together a second volume of *Videos That Teach*. We have a lot of fun working together in the same youth ministry, and we love talking and laughing during our visits to the movies. We love hearing from users of *Videos That Teach* (the first volume) expressing their thanks for the ideas and the easy-to-use format. We also love hearing how our ideas have saved youth workers time and made their teaching more effective!

In addition to the good news, we also heard some horror stories. Here's a letter from a youth worker in Louisiana named Mike:

> It was one of those crazy Wednesdays when my whole day was filled with interruptions. I didn't have the time to prepare for our evening youth group. Just minutes before the program was to start I grabbed *Videos That Teach* off my bookshelf to locate a movie clip that would help my message. After finding one, I called my wife and asked her to race the video to the church (we happened to own this particular video). She arrived within a minute of our program, and there was just no time to preview the clip. After some singing, I walked up on stage to talk, a volunteer cued the video, and I introduced the clip as we dimmed the lights.
>
> I will never forget the gasps when a certain word blurted out of the TV and into the dark room. It wasn't a horrible word, but it's not a word I would use when I'm talking to students. Thinking quickly, I actually worked it back into my message on forgiveness. My message was titled, "Things you wish you could take back" (boy, was I ever wishing I could have that one second back). I told the group about the day I had, asked for forgiveness for not previewing the movie, and silently thanked God that the pastor's son wasn't there that night.
>
> Obviously, God is sovereign, and he's bigger than one questionable word. I didn't receive one nasty phone call from a parent, but I made a commitment that night to always preview the clips. The next day, I went back and read the introduction (which I previously skipped), and I realized that you warned the readers to preview and get permission on questionable clips. Anyway, I wanted to share my story with you. Thanks for the great resource and keep working for people like me who don't have the time but need the ideas.

Learn from the experience of others. Be wise and preview each clip to be sure it meets *your* standards. Read the answer on page 20 to the question, "Why are some clips in this book from R-rated movies?"

What's different about this book?

Getting to the beginning of the clip is a little different from the first volume. Instead of putting in the cassette and having the VCR automatically set the counter to zero, fast forward to the movie logo (you'll usually see "This motion picture has been modified to fit your screen" right before the movie logo); then reset your counter to zero and fast forward to the place where the clip begins. (DVDs and subsequent video releases can have differences in the premovie trailers.)

So there I am, standing before a group of students, teaching a lesson about God's grace that I just knew would be unforgettable (after all, it took several hours to prepare—besides, it was one of those messages that would make my preaching professor proud...if he were still alive).

Halfway through my lesson two guys in the back row start smacking each other. "Knock it off, jerk!" one of them says loudly.

Of course everyone turns around to see what's happening. I put on my Wounded Puppy Dog/Semi-Stern Pastor's Frown in a desperate attempt to communicate the hurt and disappointment I feel from watching these two punks effectively kill the learning experience for everyone in the room. At the same time four girls near the front put their heads together and whisper something to each other. A guy slouching in the middle of the room yells out, "Hey, Doug, when will this sermon be over?" Then a girl from the whispering quartet runs out of the room crying.

So much for the unforgettable lesson about grace. My mind shifts to law, and I imagine sacrificing a few students on the altar of my frustration. I vow never to teach students again.

Yet within 48 hours the memories of yet another hellfest begin fading. I repress the pain of failure and begin looking (again) for fresh ways to teach next week from God's Word. Although inevitably a journey of pain and privilege, it's a journey that can be made a little easier by the book you're now holding.

Esther, Everyman, and Ever After
The ancient Hebrews told patriarchal stories. Jesus told parables. The medieval church staged morality plays. And Hollywood has become our culture's premiere storyteller. Stories, whether read, recited, or enacted, have always gripped people's imaginations and emotions.

Movies are today's parables. Theater attendance is at a record high, multiplexes are being built everywhere, and the movie industry is making more money than ever before. Even if these facts make you wince, you can still see how *Videos That Teach 2* uses movies—that is, visual storytelling—to launch meaningful discussions that go beyond the surface of the script to kids' spirits, discussions that get kids talking about themselves and life and God.

Why use movie clips in youth meetings, anyway?
Many of your students are visual learners—which means they'll be impacted more by seeing a message than by merely hearing it. And whether we like it or not, that's how most students seem to be learning these days, living as we do in a culture saturated with visual media. An incessant, 24-hour stream of images on video, TV, movies, and the Internet surround us. Teenagers tend to be

very comfortable with it all and respond well to it.

Which is why video makes perfect sense if you want to grab your students' attention.

And clips from videotaped movies are among those visual tools. For years Doug used object lessons, "spontaneous melodramas," and a variety of other creative teaching methods to reinforce his Bible teaching. He always wanted to use video clips, but could never remember the right movie at the right time for the right message. His teaching changed when Eddie James joined him at Saddleback Church in Southern California. Eddie—whose mind is a virtual storehouse of movie and video clips—would do a quick mental search on the topic Doug was to speak on, and invariably come up with a clip to use. That gift of Eddie's quickly improved Doug's teaching and the students' interest.

FAQs

• What about the copyright law?

Motion pictures are fully protected by copyright. Public exhibition, especially when an admission fee is charged, could violate copyright. The copyright doctrine of fair use, however, permits certain uses of brief excerpts from copyrighted materials for not-for-profit teaching purposes without permission. If you have specific questions about whether your plans to use film clips or other copyrighted materials in your lessons are permissible under these guidelines, you should consult your church's legal counsel. Or you or your church could apply for a blanket licensing agreement from Christian Video Licensing International <www.cvli.com> for as little as $45 per year.

• Why are some clips in this book from R-rated movies?*

Because none of the clips in *Videos That Teach 2*, even those from R-rated movies, contain language or content that is inappropriate or questionable to most youth groups.

Because clips from R movies—although the clips themselves contain no R elements—evoke very intense emotions and imagery, Schindler's List, for example.

Because sometimes, carefully, you can teach good theology by pointing to bad theology.

Because of course you'll preview whatever clip you want to use, to make sure it's appropriate for your lesson and for your group.

Because if, after you've previewed it, you're still unsure if it's suitable, you can always show it to your pastor, supervisor, or a parent for his or her opinion.

Because if you still don't feel comfortable using any of this book's 17 clips from R movies, there are still 58 clips here that are G, PG, or PG-13.

*Here are the 17 movies: *Arlington Road; Courage under Fire; Erin Brockovich; Girl, Interrupted; Gladiator; The Green Mile; The Hurricane; Instinct; The Matrix; The Messenger: The Story of Joan of Arc; Mystery, Alaska; One True Thing; Outbreak; The Patriot; Schindler's List; A Simple Plan; The Story of Us*

Because movie ratings are assigned by the dozen members or so of the ratings board of the Motion Picture Association of America <www.mpaa.org>—and the board's rating decisions are entirely subjective. Nor does the ratings board base its decisions on scriptural standards of conduct or of art. Ratings simply advise viewers about the level of "adult" content in a movie so parents can exercise appropriate control over what their underage children see.

You get the point. The use of a clip in this book does not imply endorsement of the movie in general, of other scenes in that movie in particular, of the actors' lifestyles, of the use of animals, firearms, or Scripture quotations in the movie, of the manufacturer of the cars used in the chase scenes—in short, we're not endorsing anything. This book simply lists 75 short clips, most of which (but not all of which) are appropriate and instructive to most youth groups (but not all youth groups) in most situations (but not all situations).

So you make the call. You're an adult. You're a leader of your youth group's teenagers. You know at what point instruction becomes distraction—for you, for your students, for their parents, for your church or organization. Use the summaries—and preview the clip before the lesson!—to discern which movie clips are too sophisticated for your middle schoolers, or too elementary for your senior highers. There's a lot to choose from here. Only think—before you punch the play button.

• Are you sure I need to preview a clip before showing it?
If you don't preview a clip, you're asking for trouble—at the least it may cause you embarrassment, and at the most it may cost you your job. As you probably know, youth workers lose their jobs due to oversights like this. Protect yourself—preview the clip, and cue it up precisely.

Illustrating or building a lesson with Videos That Teach 2

Most youth workers use this book one of two ways:
• You already have a lesson and want a clip to illustrate it.
Great—just flip to the "Quick Clip Locator—by topic" on page 9, find your topic, then turn to the corresponding clip. (If you're a browser, just leaf through the book with an eye on the upper right corners of the page spreads, where the topics of each clip are listed.) Or if your lesson is based on a Bible passage instead of a topic, check out the "Quick Clip Locator—by Bible reference" on page 13.
• You simply want a change of pace in this week's youth meeting—and a movie-based lesson sounds good. See the alphabetical list of movies in the table of contents for a movie you know and like, or just browse through the book until you find a clip that catches your interest.

What you'll find with each clip

Each of the 75 clips in *Videos That Teach 2* contains the same parts, clip to clip. Use as many or as few of the parts as you need to take your lesson where you want it to go. You can use just the clip to illustrate your own lesson...you can build a full-blown Bible study around the clip with the Scripture references provided (and with preliminary study on your part!)...you can trigger small-group discussions with any of several questions for each clip (with considerably less preparation). You know your students, so adapt or scavenge accordingly to meet their needs.

Here are the parts each clip includes:

Trailer

This is the leading question that gets kids' minds moving down the track of your topic (which are listed, by the way, in the upper-right corner of each clip's two-page spread). It gives you and your students an idea of what to watch and listen for as you view the clip.

For example, if you just jump into the clip of Lawrence (Michael Caine) motivating Freddy (Steve Martin) to reveal his secret plan in *Dirty Rotten Scoundrels*, all you'll get are students laughing—without paying attention to the motivation for the secret. On the other hand, if you set up your teaching time with a provocative question, students will still probably laugh at the clip—but underneath their laughter they'll get the point you're making. In fact, depending on how talkative a group you have, this opening question may trigger 15 or 20 minutes of discussion before you ever get to showing the clip.

The movie

If you're not familiar with a movie, this very brief summary helps you out. Even if you do know the movie, you can use (or read) the summary to explain the story line before you show a clip, if you want to view.

For a thorough, detailed description of the movie, get on the Web, type *movie reviews* into your favorite search engine, and choose one of the dozens of movie databases available. We found <www.empireonline.co.uk/reviews> particularly helpful. And <www.screenit.com> is "entertainment reviews for parents" of videos (and movies, music, and DVDs) that not only summarize the plot, but list in detail why the movie received the rating it did, with categories like violence, alcohol/drugs, guns/weapons, blood/gore, disrespectful/bad attitude, sex/nudity, imitative behavior, topics to talk about, and so on.

This clip

With this detailed description of the clip itself, we've also listed the start and stop times of the clip. Simply fast forward to the movie logo (you'll usually see "This motion picture has been modified to fit your screen" right before the movie logo); then reset your counter to zero and fast forward to the time where the clip begins. In case either the rental video or your VCR is different than ours, we've also included prompts from the movie—dialogue snippets or scene descriptions—to ensure that you start and stop it at the right time.

By the Book

The Bible is where you want your students to end up, sooner or later. If sooner, here's where you'll find Scriptures that are relevant to the clip's topic—to use for building a lesson from scratch or as biblical input or direction for small-group discussions.

Where to take it

Here are several discussion questions that generally try to bring together the clip's main point with the Bible passages listed earlier. Let the questions guide you, not coerce you. Tailor the questions to match the direction you want to take or to guide the depth of discussion your kids are capable of. This is the time to help them explore the meanings behind the clip, how the Bible speaks to that particular situation, and how it all applies to them.

Keep on teaching!

Trailer

How do you handle life's tough situations? Do you face them head on, or will you do *anything* to avoid dealing with them?

The movie   comedy/drama, PG-13

Gwen Cummings (Sandra Bullock) is a party girl who masks her pain by abusing alcohol and popping pills. After Gwen ruins her sister's wedding reception and destroys a front porch with a stolen limousine, the court makes her face reality by ordering her into a substance abuse treatment center. She only has 28 days to get herself cleaned up or she faces a prison sentence. She wastes the first week by keeping to herself and believing she can control her problem if she really wants to.

This clip [about 3 minutes]

▶ **Start** / 0:27:36 / "Are you coming?"

⬛ **Stop** / 0:30:55 / "This is a way to die."

Gwen's counselor (Steve Buscemi) is speaking about his past addictions. He describes how being sober between highs didn't feel very good—his skin screamed, his hands shook, and his stomach threatened to jump out of his throat. Now Gwen is fighting these same withdrawal symptoms by climbing out her third-story window to retrieve a bottle of pills she threw out earlier. What starts as a quick fix ends in added physical suffering when Gwen injures her leg and can't take painkillers.

By the Book

John 10:10; Romans 13:13; Galatians 5:19-21; Ephesians 5:18

Where to take it

● Why do people start drinking or using drugs?

● Why do some people continue to abuse alcohol and drugs when they're aware of the consequences?

● Other than abusing alcohol and drugs, what kinds of destructive behaviors do people engage in?

● Sometimes we find ourselves living a lifestyle we can't escape, even when we want to. What are some ways to break free?

● Sometimes people we care about are involved in dangerous situations and they don't know how to escape. Maybe they don't even realize how destructive their lifestyles are. How can we help them?

Angus

Trailer

What is normal? Are you normal?
Are you authentic?

The movie   comedy, PG-13

Angus Bethune (Charlie Talbert) is an overweight high school student who never seems to get a break in life, yet he notices that attractive people always seem to prosper. Life turns around when Angus finds the courage to go to the school dance and stand up for himself.

This clip

Use the first clip to set up the second.

(just over 5 minutes)

▶ **Start** / 1:12:53 / Angus walks toward Melissa.

■ **Stop** / 1:18:00 / Classmates clap for Angus and Melissa.

While Angus and Melissa (Ariana Richards) may look different on the outside, their insecurities and fears look the same on the inside. As the contrast between the homecoming queen and nerd shrinks to nothing, an unlikely but tender friendship begins.

(just under 1 minute)

▶ **Start** / 1:19:17 / "And so what...to be normal...we all have to be like you?"

■ **Stop** / 1:20:15 / "Thank God."

Angus asks what *normal* means, then points out that every person is unique and special. While conforming to others' expectations may be normal for most, it leaves little room for individuality. Living your life by others' standards prevents new voices from being heard. Instead of trying so hard to fit in, people should try to feel comfortable with themselves the way they are.

By the Book

Isaiah 64:8; 1 Corinthians 15:9-10; Ephesians 2:10

Where to take it

- Angus claims that most people walk through school never telling anyone the truth about what they really want, need, or believe because they're afraid to think for themselves. How true do you think Angus's claim is? For those who do avoid telling the truth, is fear always the reason? If not, what other reasons might there be?

- Is there only one version of "normal" at your school, or does "normal" change for different social groups? Describe what the "normal" people at your school are supposed to be like.

- How comfortable are you sharing your secrets with others? Describe the type of person you would share a secret with.

- In which situations, if any, do you feel like you can be authentic with people at your school? When do you feel like you can't be authentic? Why?

- How do you treat people who are different from you? How about the ones who annoy you?

- A lot of teen movies use characters who break the social norms but gain popularity in the end. In your experience, is this realistic? Why or why not?

- Many teenagers assume they have no power to influence their social groups at school—that they must either fit into the groups or stick out. What kind of impact do you have on the social climate of your school? What would it take to make changes?

Anywhere but Here

Trailer

Why is it so easy to love your parents and hate them at the same time?

The movie drama, PG-13

Adele August (Susan Sarandon) is tired of her comfortable life and decides to move out of her small, Midwestern city and head to glorious Beverly Hills. Her sensible and down-to-earth daughter Ann (Natalie Portman) is not excited about the move, and relocating to California just adds to the tension in their already shaky relationship. As Adele continues to embarrass and confuse her daughter by the choice she makes, Ann survives by focusing on the day when she will go to college and live her own life. But when her day of freedom finally comes, Ann learns it's not as easy to walk away from her mom as she thought it would be.

This clip (about 3 minutes)

▶ **Start** / 1:45:22 / Ann is at the ticket counter getting a boarding pass.

■ **Stop** / 1:48:35 / A long view of the busy airport terminal.

As Ann tries to say goodbye to her mother at the airport, she has some conflicting emotions. Instead of feeling relieved and grateful to be free of her mom, Ann thanks Adele for bringing them out to California in the first place. She also realizes that no matter how great the distance between them—geographically and relationally—she and her mother will always have a special bond.

● unconditional love, differences,
parent-child relationships,
growing up, saying goodbye, honor

By the Book

Psalm 27:10; Proverbs 10:1; 23:22; Luke 18:29-30; Ephesians 6:1-4

Where to take it

? When you finally leave home—to go to college, to take a job, to join the military, to get married—what emotions do you think you'll experience? How will your parents feel?

? Which of your parents' habits have you picked up? Which of their habits would you like to develop? Which ones do you intend to avoid?

? What does it mean to honor your mother and father? How can you honor them when you don't get along?

? Ann says that when her mom dies, "the world will be flat, too simple, too fair, too reasonable." What would it be like to have a parent die? Or what was it like? (Use these final questions with discretion if you have a student whose parent has died.)

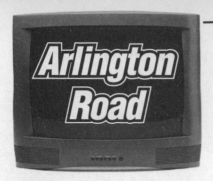

Arlington Road

Trailer

Do you feel safe?

The movie — thriller/action/drama, R

Michael Faraday (Jeff Bridges) is a college professor and widower with a nine-year-old son. His wife was an FBI agent killed in the line of duty when a routine search warrant for felony firearms turned into a two-hour siege. Michael can't forgive the FBI for the mistake that led to his wife's death and lives a guarded existence trying to protect himself and his son from more pain.

This clip (about 4 minutes)

▶ **Start** / 0:20:47 / "Fourteen months ago, on a Monday in January..."

■ **Stop** / 0:25:09 / "And still...we feel safe...because we know his name."

Michael asks his American Terrorism class the question, *"Are we really that safe?"* Michael describes a man who recently bombed a U.S. federal building as an average, friendly, moderately conservative, 30-year-old American. No one suspected he would do something like that. Michael states that after terrorist attacks occur, people want to blame someone and need to believe that the terrorist worked alone. But how likely is that? In this case they'll never know the bomber's motives because he's dead. And they won't know if he conspired with others until the terrorists strike again.

By the Book

John 10:11-15; 16:19-22, 33; Ephesians 6:10-18; 1 Thessalonians 5:2-6; Hebrews 4:12-13

Where to take it

● Why do people generally feel safe in the United States? On a scale of one (I can't watch the news—it upsets me too much) to five (this is America—what could happen?), how safe do you feel? Explain your perceptions.

● Aside from murdering someone, what are some ways that people deliberately hurt others? Without naming names, share some examples of times when people used words or actions to hurt you or someone you know. What happened?

● Why do people maliciously hurt others in order to make a point? What about those people who have no point to make?

● What could cause a normal person to lose control and seriously injure himself or others?

● What benefit, if any, does being a Christian offer you in a world that often feels unsafe?

● What are some ways you can make the world safer and more in line with God's plan for creation?

As Good as It Gets

Trailer

Do you tend to use your words as tools or weapons? Do they build others up or tear them down?

The movie — comedy/drama/romance, PG-13

Melvin Udall (Jack Nicholson) is an opinionated, obsessive-compulsive, romance novelist. He eats with plastic utensils and won't use a bar of soap twice, yet he makes it his business to point out other people's flaws. Carol Connelly (Helen Hunt), a waitress at Melvin's favorite restaurant, is the only one willing to stand up to his outbursts and irrational requests. After Melvin stands by Carol during a family medical crisis, the two begin a new relationship that changes both of their lives for the better.

This clip (5 minutes)

- ▶ **Start** / 1:36:00 / Melvin walks into the restaurant and waves.
- ■ **Stop** / 1:41:00 / "I was aiming just enough to keep you from walking out."

Melvin writes pages full of romantic imagery but can't express his feelings to Carol on their first date. Constantly tripping over his words, he manages to crush her already battered self-esteem. This is no small feat considering the fact that Carol is hiding behind the thick walls she erected years earlier to protect herself from further male rejection. When things can't get much worse, Carol asks Melvin to give her a compliment. Her tentative step toward intimacy goes a long way in saving this first date disaster.

By the Book

Romans 12:6-8; Philippians 2:1-4; 1 Timothy 5:1-3; 1 John 3:16-18

Where to take it

❓ Describe a time when you put your foot in your mouth and your words came out completely wrong.

❓ When you've said or done something wrong, how difficult is it for you to apologize? Why can apologizing be difficult?

❓ How do people tend to respond when you compliment them? How do you respond to the compliments you get from others? What's a good way to respond to compliments?

❓ Why don't people encourage and compliment each other more often?

❓ Why do you like it—or not like it—when people are vulnerable with you? Is it easier to be open with someone or to have someone open up to you? Why?

Trailer

What happens when a father and son don't see eye to eye?

The movie comedy, PG-13

Austin Powers is a parody of *James Bond* and similar 1960s spy films. Secret Agent Powers (Mike Myers) is trying to track down his nemesis Dr. Evil (also played by Myers). Both Powers and Evil were cryogenically frozen in the 1960s and thawed out in 1997. They find the modern age confusing and have difficulty acclimating.

This clip (just under 2 minutes)

- ▶ **Start** / 0:52:20 / "Okay, give in to the beauty of your feelings and say the words."

- ⏹ **Stop** / 0:54:10 / "He's quite wily, like his old man."

Dr. Evil and his son Scott (Seth Green) have spent only five days together, and there's already trouble between them. Dr. Evil has certain evil ideals that he wants his son to adopt, but Scott doesn't want to take over the world. They attend a self-help group for fathers and sons who want to understand each other. But as the unlikely pair shares their feelings with the group, it becomes obvious that Dr. Evil isn't hearing what Scott has to say.

By the Book

Matthew 5:43-47; 15:4; Luke 11:11-13; Romans 15:5-7

Where to take it

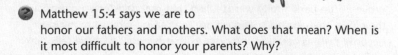

❓ Describe a time when your parents weren't listening to what you were saying. How did that make you feel? What can you do to make sure they hear and understand you next time?

❓ Why do some parents want their kids to attend the same college or choose the same career that they did? Why do children often resist following in their parents' footsteps?

❓ What do you expect from your parents? What do your parents expect from you?

❓ Which of your parents' traits would you like to see your own kids exhibit some day? Which traits do you not want to pass on to them?

❓ Matthew 15:4 says we are to honor our fathers and mothers. What does that mean? When is it most difficult to honor your parents? Why?

Trailer

What bad habits have you learned from your parents?

The movie — comedy, PG-13

Sonny Koufax (Adam Sandler) is a 30-something bachelor with little direction or ambition for his life. When social services leaves Julian, a five-year-old boy (Cole and Dylan Sprouse), on his doorstep, Sonny sees his chance to make a change. Even though his friend Kevin (Jon Stewart) is Julian's real dad, Sonny impersonates his out-of-town roommate and adopts the kid. He thinks taking care of a child will prove to his girlfriend that he's a responsible adult. She's not impressed by his instant maturity, but Sonny's experiment with fatherhood makes a lasting impression on his life.

This clip (about 1 minute)

▶ **Start** / 0:36:20 / "I know when you first got here, you thought you were going to meet your dad but..."

⏹ **Stop** / 0:37:22 / "Frankenstein!"

While at the park Sonny warns Julian that real dads often disappoint their kids, then claims that dads are the reason why so many kids become nuts as adults. Sonny shares that his own dad still tells him what to do and won't let him figure things out on his own, but Sonny promises Julian that he won't try to control him. In fact, he'll give Julian as much freedom as he wants, even letting him choose his own name—Frankenstein!

By the Book

Leviticus 26:40-42; 1 Kings 15:3; Jeremiah 11:9-10; Ezekiel 18:19-20

Where to take it

- Why did Sonny decide to let Julian do whatever he wanted to do? What's the problem with that? Why don't most parents do this?

- What are some of the responsibilities of being a parent? What happens when parents don't live up to them?

- Grade your relationship with your father or mother on a scale of one (we don't have a relationship) to 100 (we're best friends). What are some ways *you* can improve it? (Don't let this question be an opportunity for parent bashing, just a factual evaluation and ways to take personal responsibility for improving the relationship.)

- What comes to your mind when you hear the word *dad*?

- Is it easier to have a good relationship with your earthly parents or your heavenly Father? Why do you think so?

Big Momma's House

Trailer

Are you usually judgmental or compassionate toward others?

The movie — comedy/crime, PG-13

Malcolm Turner (Martin Lawrence), an undercover FBI agent, will do anything to get his man. He's been assigned to bring in a jewel thief who's trying to track down his ex-girlfriend Sherry (Nia Long). Malcolm assumes that the criminal is looking for her because she knows where the jewels are hidden. Meanwhile Sherry is on her way to visit her grandmother—Big Momma—so Malcolm stakes out Big Momma's house and waits for Sherry to show up. When Big Momma has to leave town suddenly, Malcolm sees a golden opportunity to wrap up the case. Disguising himself as the elderly woman, he waits for Sherry and the jewel thief to arrive.

This clip (just under 4 minutes)

▶ **Start** / 1:29:47 / "How do you feel Malcolm? Nervous about your testimony?"

⏹ **Stop** / 1:33:00 / Big Momma starts to sing, "Oh, Happy Day."

Malcolm decides to tell the congregation at Big Momma's church that he's sorry for his deception and the effect it had on the community—especially Sherry. Malcolm asks them not to judge him but to give him a second chance.

By the Book

Matthew 7:1-5; Mark 12:30-31; John 7:24; 1 Corinthians 5:9-13

Where to take it

❷ Malcolm says, "Don't judge me if you don't know me." Why do people tend to judge those who are different from themselves?

❷ On a scale of one (I ain't gotta clue) to 10 (I can see through skin), rate your ability to judge another person's true character. How long does it take you to figure out the kind of person she really is?

❷ What traits do you use when judging others—how they look, what they say, how they talk, how they act? What other characteristics determine whether you view someone positively or negatively?

❷ How would you explain to a new Christian what God thinks about judging others? Look up these Bible verses and any others you can think of: Matthew 7:1-5; John 7:24; 1 Corinthians 5:9-13.

❷ What do the non-Christians you know think about Christians? In their eyes, is the church a place of compassion or judgment? How do non-Christians perceive *you*?

❷ In John 7:24 Jesus says, "Stop judging by mere appearances, and make a right judgment." Describe a time when you jumped to conclusions based on something you saw or heard, but then the truth blew up in your face. If you could relive that experience, what would you do or how would you react differently?

Black Sheep

Trailer

When the pressure is on, what will people discover about you?

The movie comedy, PG-13

Mike Donnelly (Chris Farley) is the overeager and unintentionally destructive brother of popular politician Al Donnelly (Tim Matheson). Al is in a hotly contested race for governor; and he's worried that his brother Mike, whose lifestyle embarrasses him, could be a liability for his campaign. Al appoints Steve Dodds (David Spade) to watch over Mike and keep him out of the spotlight until the governor's race is over.

This clip (just under 2 minutes)

▶ **Start** / 0:59:56 / A car screeches to a stop.

■ **Stop** / 1:01:41 / "Who'd you vote for?"

Mike and Steve arrive at the polling place to cast their vote for governor. Because of his large size, Mike has some trouble getting out of the narrow voting booth and soon finds himself stuck inside. After unsuccessful attempts to exit, Mike gets angry and loses it—destroying all of the booths in order to escape. Embarrassed, Mike sheepishly turns in his ballot and quickly leaves the scene of his destructive behavior.

By the Book

Proverbs 29:11; Galatians 5:22-23; Ephesians 4:26-27; Colossians 3:8-10

Where to take it

🔧 Are you more likely to be embarrassed by your friends in front of your family or by your family in front of your friends? Why?

🔧 Describe a time when you really lost it and acted terribly toward another person. What would you do differently if you could go back and change your behavior?

🔧 Colossians 3:8-10 talks about getting rid of anger, rage, and malice. What are some of the ways you deal with your anger?

🔧 Describe someone—perhaps yourself—who seems able to make the best of any bad situation. What are some of the techniques he uses?

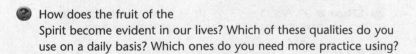

🔧 Galatians 5:22-23 lists nine great qualities that are given by the Holy Spirit to all believers. Which fruit of the Spirit did Mike display in this scene?

🔧 How does the fruit of the Spirit become evident in our lives? Which of these qualities do you use on a daily basis? Which ones do you need more practice using?

Boys and Girls

Trailer

Let's talk about sex.

The movie — comedy/romance, PG-13

Ryan (Freddie Prinze Jr.) and Jennifer (Claire Forlani) were unimpressed by each other when they first met. Their differences became more obvious in high school. Now both attend Berkeley, but they're still opposite in almost every way. In spite of this obstacle, Jennifer and Ryan manage to become close friends—maybe too close.

This clip (about 3 minutes)

▶ **Start** / 0:52:13 / "So, how did you get rid of him?"

⏹ **Stop** / 0:55:30 / "She's thinner."

As Ryan and Jennifer talk about sex and dating, male and female sexual stereotypes are debunked. Jennifer admits that having sex can be easier than making small talk with a guy. However, Ryan doesn't take sex lightly and wants to *like* a girl before he sleeps with her.

Additional Clip (about 1 minute)

This follow-up scene illustrates why some of Jennifer's choices weren't good.

▶ **Start** / 1:01:23 / "It's just that I don't think any of us know who we really are..."

⏹ **Stop** / 1:02:40 / "What if that something that we're looking for just doesn't exist?"

Jennifer asks total strangers to explain true love. She describes what she goes through when she's dating someone, all because she hopes to lose herself in a relationship to avoid being alone.

By the Book

Psalm 86:11; Proverbs 17:3; 1 Corinthians 6:18-20; Galatians 5:16-19; 1 Timothy 4:12

Where to take it

● Why is it important to establish physical boundaries in a dating relationship? What is the danger of not having any boundaries?

● Explain why it's good—or bad—to have no sexual experience before marriage. Is it realistic to expect that your future spouse will have no sexual experience? Why do you feel this way?

● What do you do to attract a member of the opposite sex? If you've ever pretended to be someone you're not, describe what happened as a result of your behavior.

● What does *true love* mean to you? If you've ever experienced this kind of love in a dating relationship, describe what it was like.

● In Psalm 86:11 David says, "Give me an undivided heart, that I may fear your name." What does this verse have to do with the topic we're discussing?

● What are some examples of things that can divide our hearts? How do divided hearts affect our relationships with God?

The Breakfast Club

Trailer

We have more in common with each other than we might think.

The movie comedy/drama, PG-13

Claire the princess (Molly Ringwald), Andrew the jock (Emilio Estevez), John the criminal (Judd Nelson), Brian the brain (Anthony Michael Hall), and Allison the basket case (Ally Sheedy) are serving a nine-hour detention. At first they seem to have nothing in common, but a day of forced interaction shows them they're not so different after all.

This clip (just under 2 minutes)

- ▶ **Start** / 1:03:05 / Andrew walks over to Allison and asks a question.

- ⏹ **Stop** / 1:04:50 / Close-up on Andrew's face as he nods his head in understanding.

Andrew asks Allison about her home life. At first she turns the conversation back to his problems, but Andrew won't let it go. Eventually she admits that her parents are the problem, and the pain of those relationships is written all over her face.

Additional Clip (about 2 minutes)

This scene gives us a glimpse of how Andrew's home life affects him.

- ▶ **Start** / 1:10:34 / "What's bizarre?

- ⏹ **Stop** / 1:13:00 / ...and explain what happened to him."

Andrew explains he's in detention because the desire for his dad's approval pushed him too far. He knows he humiliated Larry, but Andrew can only imagine how Larry felt when he told his dad what happened. Andrew's empathy for that father-son moment shows that people *can* relate to those outside of their social group by looking past stereotypes.

By the Book

1 Kings 15:3; Romans 10:12-13; 12:2-3, 16

Where to take it

- List the social groups that exist in your school. Which groups are considered cool? Which aren't?

- Describe the differences between these groups. Describe the similarities. How easy is it for someone to switch groups?

- How much interaction takes place between the different groups? Why do you think that's the case?

- What are some of the most common problems your friends have at home? What advice have you given to them? What advice would you *like* to give them?

- What are some of the benefits of talking about your pain with others? Who do you talk to the most when you're hurting? When would you consider talking to a student from another social group about your struggles?

- If you have had an opportunity to meet and talk with kids from social groups different from yours, without naming names, describe what happened and explain why it was a positive or negative experience.

Brokedown Palace

Trailer

Have you ever regretted doing the right thing?

The movie drama, PG-13

Wild and determined, Alice (Claire Danes) convinces her reserved friend Darlene (Kate Beckinsale) to go to Bangkok to celebrate their high school graduation. In the midst of their trip, an attractive Australian man befriends them and asks the girls to join him in Hong Kong. While waiting to board the plane, they're arrested for heroin smuggling and sentenced to 33 years in a hideous prison known as Brokedown Palace. Protesting their innocence, Alice and Darlene try everything within their power to get home.

This clip (about 4 minutes)

▶ **Start** / 1:28:01 / "No, no, no...get them off of me!"

⏹ **Stop** / 1:32:25 / "Let's just leave it at that."

The girls' lawyer (Bill Pullman) made a deal with the prosecutor—if the girls signed an admission of guilt, the judge would let them go home. But before the ink dries on the paper, a court official announces that drug smugglers will not be pardoned. Alice begs the judge to let Darlene go free and offers to serve both sentences—66 years in prison, which could be a life sentence for the young woman. The judge agrees, and Alice makes the ultimate sacrifice for her friend.

By the Book

Proverbs 3:3; 18:24; John 15:12-17; James 1:2-4, 12

Where to take it

- Describe a situation when you took the blame for someone or she took the blame for you.

- For what reasons might people accept responsibility for something they didn't do?

- When shouldn't people be held accountable for their actions? Or explain why you think people should always be held accountable.

- Describe your best friend. What are you willing to do for him or her? What wouldn't you do for him or her?

- Jesus said we are his friends (see John 15:14-15). What did Jesus do that supports or demonstrates this statement?

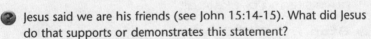

The Cable Guy

Trailer

Does your personality attract others or push them away?

The movie   comedy/drama/thriller, PG-13

After his girlfriend rejects his marriage proposal, Steven Kovacs (Matthew Broderick) moves into his own bachelor pad. When he orders cable service for his new apartment, he gets more than he bargained for—a new best friend. Chip Douglas (Jim Carrey) hooks up Steven's cable service, then tries to gain further access into his life by intruding on Steve's girlfriend, work, family, and friends. Steven just wants to get away from Chip, but pretty soon the cable guy is stalking him.

This clip (about 4 minutes)

▶ **Start** / 0:19:20 / Scene starts with some guys playing basketball.

⏹ **Stop** / 0:23:30 / "I gotta shower and do some stuff anyway."

Chip finds Steve playing a pick-up game of basketball with his friends. Steve is reluctant to let Chip join in, but finally relents. It's soon obvious that Chip is a little more than aggressive when he becomes downright nasty on the court. The game ends when Chip suddenly finds himself alone, and he only has himself and his competitive nature to blame.

By the Book

Luke 6:27-36; 11:5-8; Romans 2:1-6; 9:22-25; Galatians 6:7-10

Where to take it

How important are friends in your life? Describe what you do to maintain your friendships and the work it involves.

Without naming names, describe a time when a friend became jealous of your other relationships. Why is it important for friends to give each other some space—time to be alone or to hang out with other friends or family?

Why do some people always have to win or to be right—even with their friends? Why do people find it difficult to lose or to be wrong about something?

If you've ever been involved in a one-sided relationship like Steven and Chip's, without naming names, explain what happened with this person and how you felt about the situation. Why weren't your feelings for each other mutual?

If you're in a situation similar to Steven's right now, what are some ways you can "love your enemies," like the Bible advises us to do in Luke 6:27-36?

Chariots of Fire

Trailer

How do you respond to temptation and the pressure to conform?

The movie   drama, PG

This is the true story of two men training to run in the 1924 Olympics. Both love to run, but they do it for different reasons. Eric Liddell (Ian Charleson) incorporates his Christian beliefs into all that he does, believing that the power to finish the race comes from within and a commitment to Christ helps him run straight. But Harold Abrahams (Ben Cross) runs as a weapon against being Jewish. When Harold wins a race, he believes Jews don't appear so inferior, and he finally feels accepted by the world around him.

This clip (about 3 minutes)

▶ **Start** / 1:26:50 / "Your Royal Highness, may I present Mr. Eric Liddel."

⏹ **Stop** / 1:30:13 / "Sir, God knows I love my country; but I can't make that sacrifice."

The Prince of Wales and members of the Olympics Committee meet with Eric to try to convince him to set aside his beliefs and run his race on the Sabbath. Eric doesn't like their reasons and resents their suggestion that he's not being loyal to his king or his country by sitting this one out. Despite the great pressure the men put on him, Eric stands firmly behind his decision to obey God's law.

By the Book

Exodus 20:8-11; Mark 3:1-5; Luke 21:14-19; Romans 14:5;
Colossians 2:16-17; 3:16-17

Where to take it

2 In your opinion is Eric's position extremist, admirable, or a little of both? Why?

2 Why is it easy or hard for you to share with others what you believe about God and Christianity?

2 When have you been tempted to go against your beliefs? Or describe a time when you've seen others tempted to do so.

2 Do you have any convictions that you would *never* go against? What are they? Have these convictions ever been tested? What happened?

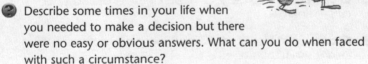

2 Describe some times in your life when you needed to make a decision but there were no easy or obvious answers. What can you do when faced with such a circumstance?

The Cider House Rules

Trailer

What does it feel like to be forgotten?

The movie drama, PG-13

Homer Wells (Tobey Maguire) spent his childhood in an orphanage, growing up under the tender care and instruction of Dr. Wilbur Larch (Michael Caine). Now the young man assists Dr. Larch with the responsibilities of caring for all the orphan children, often from the time they are born, at the orphanage. Homer doesn't always agree with Dr. Larch's opinions, and he wants to see the world. Eventually Dr. Larch has no choice but to let Homer go discover the truth for himself.

This clip (2 minutes)

- ▶ **Start** / 13:42 / A car drives up to the orphanage.

- ■ **Stop** / 15:43 / "Only the right people can have you."

In this scene a married couple adopts a little girl from the orphanage. As the new family drives away, Curly (Spencer Diamond) sadly watches them go. It's not the first time the young boy has been overlooked by potential parents. He wonders why no one wants to take him home to live with them. Homer assures Curly that his life is not a mistake when he says, "You're one of the best, and we wouldn't let just anyone take you."

By the Book

Deuteronomy 4:29-31; Psalm 68:5-6; Jeremiah 29:11-14;
Luke 12:6-7; Hebrews 12:5-11

Where to take it

● Describe a time when you felt abandoned or left behind.

● Suppose a couple gets pregnant but they aren't ready to have children. List the pros and cons for each of the following decisions—abortion, adoption, keeping the child.

● Describe a situation in which you think it would be best for an unmarried couple to keep a child. Now describe a situation in which you think it would be best for a couple to give the child up for adoption. Is there a time when abortion is the best option? Talk about your thoughts.

● What does it mean to describe yourself as a child of God? What are the benefits of being his child? What are the drawbacks?

● What does the phrase *God is our heavenly parent* mean to you?

● Read Deuteronomy 4:29-31; Psalm 68:5-6; Jeremiah 29:11-14; Luke 12:6-7; and Hebrews 12:5-11. How do these verses illustrate the ways in which God acts like a parent to us?

● What are the similarities between how God views or treats you and the way your parents do? What are the differences?

53

Courage under Fire

Trailer

Is confession really good for the soul?

The movie
drama/war/mystery, R

Lieutenant Colonel Serling (Denzel Washington) is assigned to find out information about the rescue of a downed helicopter crew during the Gulf War. The army wants to know if Medivac pilot Captain Karen Walden (Meg Ryan) deserves the Medal of Honor for saving the crewmembers' lives. Meanwhile, a newspaper reporter (Scott Glenn) is investigating Serling's involvement in a wartime incident where one American tank fired upon another. The reporter's questions force Serling to wrestle with some demons from his own tour of duty in the desert.

This clip (just under 3 minutes)

▶ **Start** / 1:43:45 / Denzel Washington picks up an army pendant.

⏹ **Stop** / 1:46:32 / "Thank you, sir."

Since his return to the States, Serling has been trying to put the past behind him by working long hours and drinking too much. When he realizes his pain management methods aren't helping anybody, Serling faces the truth and makes a startling confession about how his good friend Tom died during the war. Serling asks Tom's parents to forgive him for covering up his deadly mistake and for allowing the Army to do the same. Once he's put his burden down, Lt. Colonel Serling can start living again.

By the Book

Psalm 32:1-5; 55:22; Proverbs 28:13; Isaiah 46:4; Matthew 11:28-30; 18:21-22; 2 Corinthians 2:5-8; Galatians 6:1-2; Colossians 3:12-14

Where to take it

🙂 Lt. Colonel Serling says he can't ask Tom's parents to forgive him for how their son died. Tom's dad says, "But it's a burden you're going to have to put down sometime." What does that mean?

🙂 Read Psalm 32:1-5; 55:22; Isaiah 46:4; Matthew 11:28-30; and Galatians 6:1-2. How can we let go of the burden of our struggles?

🙂 On a scale of one (painfree) to 10 (excruciating), rate how easy it is for you to forgive someone when they ask you to do so. How about when they *don't* ask for your forgiveness? If there is a difference between these two ratings, explain why.

🙂 On a scale of one (painfree) to 10 (excruciating), how easy is it for you to ask someone to forgive *you*? If this rating is much higher or lower than the two previous ratings, explain why.

🙂 Read Matthew 18:21-22; 2 Corinthians 2:5-8; Colossians 3:12-14; and any other passages you can think of about forgiveness. What does the Bible say about it?

Dirty Rotten Scoundrels

Trailer

What's it like to live with secrets?

The movie comedy, PG

Freddy Benson (Steve Martin) and Lawrence Jamieson (Michael Caine) are two con-artists who make their money by manipulating gullible, wealthy women along the Riviera. Freddy and Lawrence compete for the attention of an heiress named Janet Colgate (Glenn Headly), but in the end Janet is not the innocent dove she first appeared to be.

This clip (about 4 minutes)

▶ **Start** / 0:59:40 / Freddy is standing and looking around the hotel room.

■ **Stop** / 1:04:15 / The scene ends with Freddy's tears of pain.

Freddy is trying to swindle money from Janet by pretending to be confined to a wheelchair. When Lawrence gets wind of Freddy's con, he decides to unearth his pal's secret by using some painful techniques. Freddy valiantly tries to keep up the lie even though the pain becomes unbearable.

By the Book

Proverbs 27:5-6; Matthew 7:1-5; 18:15-17; 2 Thessalonians 3:14-15;
1 Peter 2:1

Where to take it

● What's the longest you've ever kept a secret? How hard was it to keep? What was the outcome for you and for others because of this secret?

● What should you do if someone tells you a secret (like a suicide plan or sexual abuse) that you know you shouldn't keep because they'll be harmed if you do?

● When do you feel it's appropriate to challenge someone's lifestyle or hold her accountable for her actions?

● Read Matthew 7:1-5; 18:15-17; and 2 Thessalonians 3:14-15. What does the Bible say about holding someone accountable?

● List the people you'd feel comfortable confronting about their mistakes. What's their typical response when you talk to them this way?

● If it's true for you, describe why you think it's important to have people in your life who hold you accountable for your actions and beliefs.

● Name some people who aren't afraid to tell you when you've messed up. Explain why you do—or don't—appreciate their efforts to keep you in line.

Trailer

Would you like to participate on a reality TV show?

The movie comedy, PG-13

True TV is a cable channel that shows documentaries all day, every day—with low ratings. In an effort to bring back the viewers, the program director (Ellen DeGeneres) proposes they host a contest. The grand-prize winner will get big money, and True TV will get to film the winner's life 24 hours a day for one month—unedited. When Ed Pekurny (Matthew McConaughey), a San Francisco video store clerk, is declared the winner, it seems like a win-win situation. But Ed eventually discovers that fame and popularity aren't what he expected.

This clip (just under 3 minutes)

- ▶ **Start** / 1:37:05 / "Uh, not too good. No, you see that's why it states very specifically in your contract..."

- ⏹ **Stop** / 1:40:02 / Ed runs in front of a trolley full of screaming fans.

Ed's status as a cultural icon loses its appeal when it interferes with his work, his family, and his relationship with Shari (Jenna Elfman). When the network executives tell him they plan to extend the length of the program, Ed learns that his contract won't let him escape the fishbowl existence he's endured for nearly four months. Can he find a way to regain his privacy and salvage the relationships that have been scarred by EDtv?

By the Book

Job 13:9; Psalm 49:16-20; 103:15-16; 139:7-12; Proverbs 5:21-23; Mark 8:34-37; 12:30; Luke 12:15-21; 16:15; James 4:4

Where to take it

- Describe the good and bad aspects of being famous. In light of the pros and cons, would you like to be famous? Explain your reasoning.

- Read Psalm 49:16-20; 103:15-16; Mark 8:34-37; 12:30; Luke 12:15-21; and James 4:4. What does the Bible say about the pursuit of fame, fortune, and popularity?

- Why is our culture so fascinated by watching people live their lives on reality television shows? What statements does this make about our society?

- Explain why you would or would not let a camera follow you 24/7.

- If a camera did follow you, what would people see? Would people be surprised by what they saw? Why?

- What would you change about your lifestyle if you knew your parents were watching? Your friends? Your church?

- Chances are slim that you'll appear on a reality TV show some day, but someone is watching you 24/7. Read Psalm 139:7-12; Proverbs 5:21-23; and Luke 16:15. How does it impact you to realize that God sees everything you do all day long?

- Do you care about God's perception of you to the same degree that you care about what your parents or friends think? Explain.

Trailer

How do you continue to trust God when times are tough?

The movie drama, R

This movie is based on the true story about a research assistant and single mother of three, Erin Brockovich (Julia Roberts). Erin convinces her boss, Ed Masry (Albert Finney), to pursue a lawsuit against a large utility company in Hinkley, California. The company is being blamed for contaminating the local water supply and causing an outbreak of cancer and other serious physical problems among the residents of this small community. The more information she digs up about the case, the more time she spends away from home and her family. The work she's doing could help right a wrong and improve people's lives, but at what personal cost for Erin?

This clip (just under 2 minutes)

- ▶ **Start** / 1:09:53 / A phone is ringing in the bedroom.

- ■ **Stop** / 1:11:43 / Scene goes to black.

Erin calls home and learns that her youngest child said her first word. Erin is excited about her daughter's milestone but feels conflicted. Her paychecks provide for her family, and her work provides her with a self-confidence she's never experienced before. Yet the pain of missing her daughter's first words is enough to make her question if she's doing the right thing for her family.

By the Book

Proverbs 31:10-31; Haggai 1:5-9; 2 Thessalonians 3:6-10;
1 Timothy 5:8

Where to take it

● What things or events can cause people to miss out on important moments in life?

● Describe a time when you missed a special event in someone else's life. How did you deal with it?

● If you've ever lived in a single parent home, do you think your mom or dad ever felt like Erin did in this scene? How can you help your mom or dad in situations like this?

● If you're a single parent, how did watching this scene make you feel? Can you relate to Erin's emotions? If you feel comfortable doing so, share your story with the group. What have been the advantages of being a single parent? What are the disadvantages?

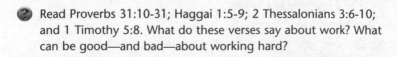

● Read Proverbs 31:10-31; Haggai 1:5-9; 2 Thessalonians 3:6-10; and 1 Timothy 5:8. What do these verses say about work? What can be good—and bad—about working hard?

● List the five most important values in your life, and explain why you chose them.

● Describe how you prioritize your life around your top five values and how you make choices based on them.

61

Ever After

Trailer

What's left when trust is taken away from a relationship?

The movie romance, PG

For 10 years, Danielle (Drew Barrymore) has worked for her cruel stepmother Rodmilla (Anjelica Huston) and catered to her spoiled stepsisters. During an encounter with Prince Henry (Dougray Scott), Danielle lets him believe she's a noble woman, and he begins to pursue her. Their relationship blossoms until Rodmilla announces the truth at Henry's engagement party.

This clip (just under 2 minutes)

▶ **Start** / 1:35:19 / "Have you any idea what that girl went through to get here tonight?"

⏹ **Stop** / 1:36:55 / Danielle is sitting and crying in the rain.

Before Danielle could explain her side of the story, Henry publicly condemned and dismissed her. Leonardo da Vinci confronts the prince about his prideful behavior, but Henry doesn't want to listen. Danielle's deceit deeply wounded him, and he believes her love for him was also a lie.

Additional Clip (just under 3 minutes)

▶ **Start** / 1:46:22 / Danielle walks out of the castle.

⏹ **Stop** / 1:49:10 / Henry and Danielle hold each other.

After the party, Rodmilla sold Danielle to a neighbor to help pay her debts. Prince Henry goes to rescue and apologize to Danielle. When

he finds her, not only has Danielle already freed herself, but she's also wary of the prince's intentions. Henry assures her that he loves her for who she is and that she is his match in every way.

By the Book

Psalm 139:13-16; Proverbs 13:10; John 3:16; Romans 5:8;
Ephesians 2:4-10; 4:25-27; Colossians 3:12-14; James 1:19-20

Where to take it

- Da Vinci tells Henry, "A life without love is no life at all." Explain this sentence in your own words and whether or not you agree with it.

- Explain what the above quote means as it's rewritten here, "A life without God's love is no life at all." If you need help, look at John 3:16; Romans 5:8; Ephesians 2:4-10; and any other Scripture you can think of that relates to God's love for us.

- Da Vinci says that if Prince Henry won't yield, he doesn't deserve Danielle. What does this mean?

- Read Proverbs 13:10; Ephesians 4:25-27; and James 1:19-20. What could Prince Henry learn by reading these passages? If he had read them before the party that night, how might he have reacted differently to the truth about Danielle?

- Describe a time in your life when pride kept you from experiencing the very best.

- In the second scene, why does Danielle take such delight in hearing Henry say her name? What does it mean to you when someone knows your name? What about when they don't?

- Read Psalm 139:13-16. Explain what it means to know that God made you the way he did on purpose and that he knows all about you and loves you, inside and out. Is it reassuring? Do you wish he'd made you differently in some ways?

- What does it take to live happily ever after? Which of these requirements do Henry and Danielle exhibit in this last scene?

First Knight

Trailer

What does it mean to serve and love someone with all your heart?

The movie — action/adventure/drama/romance, PG-13

In the tale of Camelot, King Arthur (Sean Connery), Sir Lancelot (Richard Gere), and Queen Guinevere (Julia Ormond) are each forced to make decisions based on bravery, loyalty, and love. King Arthur is getting older and looking for another knight to add to his Round Table. Lancelot is the obvious choice, but he's hesitant to commit. Their story questions what it means to truly serve and love another person.

This clip (just under 4 minutes)

▶ **Start** / 0:44:31 / King Arthur and Lancelot enter the room containing the Round Table.

■ **Stop** / 0:48:10 / "I may be wrong."

King Arthur questions Lancelot about his current commitments and discovers that the knight doesn't have much in his life—things or people—to hold him back. Not only does this unfettered lifestyle prevent Lancelot from getting hurt emotionally, but it also helps him to stay sharp as a knight, protecting him physically. King Arthur challenges Lancelot to think about what he should be serving and the one mission that's worth fighting for.

By the Book

Matthew 25:14-30; Mark 9:33-35; 2 Corinthians 3:17-18;
Galatians 5:13-15; Ephesians 6:7-8; Philippians 2:3-11; 1 Peter 2:16-17

Where to take it

- King Arthur tells Lancelot, "A man who fears nothing, loves nothing. A man who loves nothing, has no joy." The next logical step is "A man who fears nothing, has no joy." Explain why you agree or disagree with these statements.

- What are the pros and cons of living without any commitments like Lancelot?

- What are the pros and cons of being fully committed to someone or something?

- In this scene Lancelot reads part of the Round Table credo: "In serving each other, we become free." Explain what that statement means.

- What does it mean to have freedom in Christ? Look up 2 Corinthians 3:17-18; Galatians 5:13-15; and 1 Peter 2:16-17 to give you some ideas.

- What does the Bible say about serving others? Read Mark 9:33-35; Ephesians 6:7-8; and Philippians 2:3-11.

- What do you find easy about serving others? What do you find hard?

- Read the parable of the talents found in Matthew 25:14-30. What is the meaning of this parable? Which of the three servants do you relate to? How are you like that servant?

- Make a list of your spiritual gifts and talents. Which ones are you regularly using to serve others? Which ones could you be using to help people? What's stopping you?

Forces of Nature

Trailer

Are you supposed to spend the rest of your life with just one person?

The movie comedy/romance, PG-13

In two days Ben Holmes (Ben Affleck) is supposed to marry Bridget Cahill (Maura Tierny). When his plane skids off the runway in New York, Ben helps the woman sitting next to him. Bad weather means flying home that night is no longer an option for Ben, so to thank him for saving her life, Sarah (Sandra Bullock) offers to help him get to Georgia. They travel by bus, rental car, and train—all with further complications—but after spending only 48 hours together, Ben questions his decision to marry Bridget.

This clip (4 minutes)

- ▶ **Start** / 1:33:50 / Ben walks toward the house as the wind blows chaos all around him.

- ⏹ **Stop** / 1:37:50 / Ben and Bridget kiss.

After arriving in Savannah in one piece, Ben must decide whether to go ahead and marry Bridget or begin a new relationship with Sarah. When the bride and groom finally meet in the midst of a hurricane, Ben realizes that nothing can destroy his feelings for Bridget. After all he's been through during the past two days, he knows that no matter what comes their way, they'll survive if they face it together.

By the Book

Deuteronomy 23:21-23; Proverbs 5:18; 20:6; Ecclesiastes 5:2-5; Song of Songs 8:6-7; Matthew 5:36-37; Ephesians 5:28-33

Where to take it

- Does the fact that Ben questioned his decision to marry Bridget make him unfaithful to her? Explain why you think so.

- On a scale of 23 (energizing) to 79 (exhausting), how hard do you think it is to remain faithful to someone? Why do you feel this way?

- This movie assumes there is only one right person in this world for you—your soul mate. Describe why you agree or disagree with this perspective.

- If you agree, what should you do if you're already married when you meet "the right one"? What does the Bible say you should do? (See Proverbs 5:18; Song of Songs 8:6-7; Ephesians 5:28-31; and other passages you can think of.)

- Talk about what the Bible says about making a vow. Read Deuteronomy 23:21-23; Ecclesiastes 5:2-5; Matthew 5:36-37; and other verses you find that relate to this issue.

- If you were to write your marriage vows right now, what would be the most important things to include?

Forever Young

Trailer

What kind of example do you set for others?

The movie — adventure/romance/science fiction, PG

The doctors didn't think his girlfriend would awake from her coma, and Captain Daniel McCormick (Mel Gibson) didn't think he could live without her, so the test pilot agreed to be cryogenically frozen for a military science experiment. However, when the project is abandoned, Daniel is forgotten until fifty years later when Nat Cooper (Elijah Wood) unwittingly starts the thawing process. With his body temperature back to a healthy 98.6 degrees, Daniel befriends Nat and teaches him some lessons about life and love.

This clip (just under 4 minutes)

▶ **Start** / 1:08:52 / "Nat?"

⏹ **Stop** / 1:12:18 / Girl smiles and shuts the window shade.

Nat likes a girl in his class named Alice (Veronica Lauren). Daniel doesn't want Nat to miss his chance, so he advises the boy to tell Alice how he feels the next time he sees her. That night Nat climbs a tree outside Alice's window and sings a heartfelt rendition of "You Are My Sunshine." When her dad comes to the window in the middle of his serenade, Nat shares his true feelings. His brave admission does more to impress the girl than if he'd finished the song.

By the Book

Proverbs 16:20; 19:20; 1 Corinthians 13:4-7; Ephesians 4:22-25; 1 Timothy 4:12

Where to take it

2 What is your definition of true love?

2 What's God's definition of true love? Look at 1 Corinthians 13:4-7 for help.

2 Do your parents or other adults take your dating relationships seriously? Explain why you think this way.

2 What do you do when you want to attract someone of the opposite sex? How does it compare to Daniel's advice?

2 What advice about dating or love do you get from your parents? Do you follow their advice about love relationships? Why or why not? If your parents don't give you any advice about this topic, explain why you think that's the case.

2 In 1 Timothy 4:12, Paul shares five areas in which youths should try to set a good example for other believers—list them here. Which of these are your strongest areas and which are your weakest?

2 What areas from 1 Timothy 4:12 did Nat exemplify in this clip? How do you think his behavior affected Alice? Her father? Daniel?

2 How could your life impact other people's behavior or attitudes in these five areas? Who do you think you impact the most? Who do you impact the least? Explain why you feel that way.

Trailer

What impact does divorce have on children?

The movie drama/romance, PG-13

Billy Chapel (Kevin Costner) is reaching the end of his baseball career. While pitching a perfect game at Yankee Stadium, Chapel's thoughts race back and forth between his life as a professional athlete and the challenges of falling in love with Jane (Kelly Preston) and trying to build a life with one person.

This clip (just under 3 minutes)

▶ **Start** / 1:03:10 / "You want something? I'll have a V-8."

■ **Stop** / 1:05:50 / "And now it's like...she doesn't believe in it."

Billy picks up Jane's daughter, Heather, and takes her home. Heather (Jena Malone) ran away to her father's house because she thought her mother was too overbearing. Billy gets an earful as Heather opens up on the plane ride home. She shares her perspective on her mom and dad, explains how she knows which parent really cares about her, and admits that she makes wrong choices based on this knowledge. Her confessions cause Billy to reevaluate whether kids and marriage are right for him at this stage in the game.

By the Book

Proverbs 20:11; 23:22; Matthew 19:3-11; 1 Corinthians 7:27-28; Ephesians 6:1-4; Hebrews 13:4

Where to take it

❓ Young children expect their parents to be perfect. Explain why you do or don't expect perfection from your parents.

❓ Why do children resist learning from their parents' mistakes, choosing to figure things out on their own instead? In what areas of your life do you trust your parents' advice? In what areas do you choose to go your own way and make your own mistakes?

❓ Why do you find it easy or hard to follow your parents' advice? Explain why you believe that not listening to your parents is a good or bad choice to make.

❓ How has divorce affected you or your friends?

❓ If your parents are divorced, in what ways has it changed their lives? How has it changed the way you relate to your parents?

❓ If your parents are not divorced, describe the positive and negative effects of divorce that you've witnessed in other adults and kids you know.

❓ Over half of all marriages end in divorce—even in the Christian population. What are the ingredients for a successful relationship?

Forrest Gump

Trailer

How far would you go for a friend?

The movie — adventure/drama/comedy, PG-13

Despite growing up during a time in history when the American people lost their idealism, Forrest Gump (Tom Hanks) maintained a sense of innocence and fierce loyalty to his friends and family. After enlisting in the Army, Forrest met "Bubba" Blue (Mykelti Williamson). They served in the Vietnam War together and became best friends. All Bubba could talk about was becoming the captain of a shrimping boat, and Forrest helped make Bubba's dream a reality.

This clip (just under 3 minutes)

▶ **Start** / 0:54:14 / Forrest is running through the jungle.

■ **Stop** / 0:56:50 / "That's all I have to say about that."

Forrest is running for his life in the Vietnam jungle. When he reaches the rest of his platoon, Forrest sees that Bubba is missing. With no thought for his own safety, Forrest heads back into the jungle amidst whirring bullets and fiery explosions to find his friend.

Additional Clip (just under 2 minutes)

▶ **Start** / 1:41:46 / "Didn't you say that you were waiting for the number seven bus?"

■ **Stop** / 1:43:21 / "I cut that grass for free."

Forrest describes how the proceeds from the Bubba Gump Shrimp enterprise grew so large that he never had to worry about money again. So he gave most of the money away, sending Bubba's portion to the Blue family. Forrest's unselfish act exemplifies his undying loyalty to his good friend.

By the Book

1 Samuel 18:1-4; 20:41-42; Luke 5:17-26; Philippians 1:20; 1 John 3:16-18

Where to take it

❓ Read the account in Luke 5:17-26. How do you suppose the friends felt about the man on the mat? What did they want Jesus to do?

❓ Read 1 Samuel 18:1-4 and 20:41-42 describing the friendship between David and Jonathan. Why is it important to have close friends? List some of the things your close friends do for you.

❓ What would you be willing to risk or sacrifice in order to help a friend? What wouldn't you be willing to do for a friend? Why?

❓ What parts of your life are easy to talk about with your friends? Which are more difficult to talk about?

❓ On a scale of one (I can't keep my mouth shut) to 10 (my lips are super-glued shut.) rate how hard it is for you to talk to your friends about God? Why is this the case?

❓ If you have friends who don't attend church or aren't Christians, describe the ways you've shared God's love with them. In what positive or negative ways do your differing beliefs affect your friendship?

Frequency

Trailer

When was the last time you had a good talk with God?

The movie   thriller/science fiction, PG-13

When John Sullivan (James Caviezel) was a boy, his firefighter father (Dennis Quaid) was killed while rescuing a child from a burning building. Thirty years later John still misses his dad terribly. While playing with his dad's old ham radio one night, John somehow manages to contact Frank back in 1969. John warns Frank about the fire that killed him and saves his dad's life. However, this change in historical events unexpectedly puts his mother's life in jeopardy. Now with 30 years still separating them, father and son must work together to save John's mother.

This clip   (about 6 minutes)

▶ **Start** / 0:47:15 / "Hello? Hello?"

■ **Stop** / 0:53:20 / Scene ends on Frank's face.

On the anniversary of Frank's death, John and his dad are talking on the ham radio and catching up on everything from John's career to sports and the future of technology. Frank promises he won't die on the job that night, leaving his son without a father like he did when John was six. Yet both men are reluctant to get off the airwaves, afraid they won't have a chance to talk like this again.

By the Book

1 Kings 8:22-26, 54-60; Psalm 5:1-3; Matthew 6:5-13;
Ephesians 6:18; 1 John 3:1-2

Where to take it

(?) Describe a time when God seemed to speak to you through the words or actions of another person. How did you react or respond?

(?) On a scale from one (God who?) to 10 (God and I are inseparable), how would you rate your relationship with God? What things have led to the current state of your relationship with the Lord?

(?) On the same scale as above, rate where you'd like your relationship with God to be a year from now. What about in five years? What can you start doing today to receive a better rating down the road?

(?) What do you guess—or know—other people do to improve their relationships with God? What does God need to do?

(?) Describe a time when you've been passionate about spending time with God. If you haven't had this experience before, describe something you *are* passionate about—a hobby, a class, a future career, a musical instrument. List the things you do to keep your interest alive and passionate. How can you apply these same principles and techniques to become more passionate about spending time with the Lord?

Galaxy Quest

Trailer

Who is the real you?

The movie — action/adventure/comedy/ science fiction, PG

Captain Peter Quincy Taggart was a character on the now-defunct television series *Galaxy Quest*. However, a group of zealous sci-fi fans keep the old series alive by dutifully attending personal appearances made by Jason Nesmith (Tim Allen), the actor who played Taggart, and his crew. Little did they know that a group of aliens have also been watching the show and copying everything from the costumes and culture to the design of their space ship. When Quellek (Patrick Breen), a despotic green villain, threatens to annihilate them, the aliens know only Captain Taggart can save them.

This clip (just under 5 minutes)

▶ **Start** / 1:01:55 / "Jason, thank God...you are alive."

■ **Stop** / 1:06:35 / "I am so sorry."

The scene shows Jason speaking to the alien leader Mathesar (Enrico Colantoni), as Quellek holds the ship and crew hostage. Quellek forces Jason to tell Mathesar that he has been lying. Mathesar doesn't understand until Jason says in the simplest of terms that neither Captain Taggart nor his crew is real, they're just actors who pretend for a living. As Mathesar realizes no one can save his people now, his hope dies while Jason's integrity begins.

By the Book

Psalm 34:11-14; Proverbs 17:20; 26:18-19; 2 Corinthians 4:2;
Ephesians 5:6-11

Where to take it

🤔 Mathesar built his whole life around a fake world. Describe how
some people build their lives around falsehoods today.

🤔 Why is it important for friends to be honest with each other?

🤔 What does the Bible say about lies and truth? Read Psalm
34:11-14; Proverbs 17:20; 26:18-19; 2 Corinthians 4:2;
Ephesians 5:6-11; and other verses you can think of.

🤔 What comparisons can you
make between the
possible consequences of
Jason's lies and those that
were mentioned in the
above passages?

🤔 Describe a situation
when you told a
loved one that you
lied to him. How
did he respond to
your honesty?
What happened to
the level of trust
between you?

Do you believe in ghosts?

The movie — comedy/romance/thriller, PG-13

Everything changed the night that Sam (Patrick Swayze) and his girlfriend Molly (Demi Moore) were mugged in an alley. As Sam bravely struggled to take away the attacker's gun, he was shot and killed, leaving Molly to face a life of loneliness without him. Meanwhile, Sam's spirit is stuck wandering the earth until he figures out why he was killed and makes sure Molly is safe. Oda Mae Brown (Whoopi Goldberg) is the only person that can see or hear him, and she reluctantly agrees to help Sam investigate his murder.

This clip (just under 6 minutes)

▶ **Start** / 1:55:06 / A man's spirit leaves his dead body.

⏹ **Stop** / 2:00:56 / The scene fades to black.

Carl (Tony Goldwyn) doesn't yet realize that the only reason he can see Sam's spirit is because Carl is also dead. After discovering his own body lying across the windowsill, Carl stares at Sam in shock. But before the two can say anything, dark spirits growl and slither into the room to escort Carl's spirit off to hell. Then Sam says his goodbyes to Molly and Oda Mae before heading toward the light of heaven.

By the Book

Luke 12:4-5; John 14:2-4; 2 Peter 2:4-9; Jude 5-7;
Revelation 7:15-17; 20:12-15

Where to take it

❓ Explain why you do or don't believe in ghosts.

❓ One of the last lines in the clip says, "It's amazing Molly. The
love inside...you take it with you." What do you think this
statement means?

❓ What, if anything, will you take with you to heaven?

❓ *The road to hell is paved with good intentions.* Explain what this
saying means and why you agree or disagree with it.

❓ Read John 14:2-4; 2 Peter 2:4-9; Jude 5-7; Revelation 7:15-17;
20:12-15; and other passages that mention heaven or hell.
Describe how heaven and hell are portrayed in the Bible.

❓ Does our society trivialize heaven and hell or
put too much emphasis on them, or is there
a good balance? Why do you think is so?

Girl, Interrupted

Trailer

Are you achieving your goals in life?

The movie drama, R

Girl, Interrupted is based on the true story of Susanna Kaysen (Winona Ryder), a young woman who commits herself to a psychiatric institute after a suicide attempt in the 1960s. Susanna immediately looks up to Lisa (Angelina Jolie), a patient who proudly displays her sociopathic behavior and enjoys breaking the rules. Pretty soon Susanna sees that Lisa is not a good role model of recovery for her. After getting some distance between them, Susanna finally realizes that if she wants to find peace, she has to face herself.

This clip (just under 3 minutes)

▶ **Start** / 1:12:50 / "You know, I have a problem coping with this hospital. I want to leave."

⏹ **Stop** / 1:15:24 / "For now."

Susanna meets with Dr. Wick (Vanessa Redgrave), the head counselor in the ward, who asks her some tough questions about the lack of progress she's been making in her treatment. Susanna pretends indifference, but Dr. Wick isn't fooled. The counselor tells Susanna that she has some big questions to answer about herself and even bigger decisions to make about her future. Susanna begins to see that she is the greatest obstacle on the road to recovery.

By the Book

Proverbs 16:1-3, 9; 19:20; 21:30; James 1:5-8

Where to take it

🙋 Explain why decision making is easy or hard for you.

🙋 Are your friends open to talking with you about major decisions in their lives? If not, how can you make yourself more receptive to them?

🙋 Read Proverbs 16:1-3, 9; 19:20; 21:30; and James 1:5-8. How do these verses comfort you or help you relax when making decisions for the future?

🙋 What are some big questions that you have about life? Who do you feel most comfortable talking to about these questions?

🙋 Do you usually pray about *all* the decisions you need to make? Just the big decisions? Just the little ones? What has been the result of your prayers?

Gladiator Trailer

How do you want to be remembered?

The movie — drama/action, R

Commodus (Joaquin Phoenix) takes the Roman throne by force and orders the execution of Maximus (Russell Crowe), the late emperor's trusted general. Maximus escapes death but finds his wife and son murdered. Sold as a gladiator, Maximus channels his hatred and wins every battle, earning the respect of his fellow gladiators and the favor of Roman audiences. The longer Maximus lives, the greater his opportunity for revenge.

This clip (about 5 minutes)

▶ **Start** / 0:22:22 / "You sent for me, Caesar?"

⏹ **Stop** / 0:27:56 / "And bring an old man another blanket."

Caesar laments his final legacy is one full of bloodshed. He feels Rome is not what it used to be, nor what it *should* be, and plans to leave someone in charge to give power back to the people. Caesar believes Maximus is the right man for the job.

Additional Clip (about 3 minutes)

▶ **Start** / 0:32:15 / "Are you ready to do your duty for Rome?"

⏹ **Stop** / 0:35:38 / "I would butcher the whole world if only you'd love me."

Commodus learns that his father has not chosen him to take over the Roman throne. As he shares his feelings of rejection with his father, it's obvious that Caesar's legacy as a parent is also a failure. Caesar takes full blame for the trouble between him and his son, but it's too little too late.

By the Book

Jeremiah 29:11-14; 1 Corinthians 9:24-27; Galatians 5:22-26;
James 3:13-18; 1 Peter 1:3-7; 5:2-9; 2 Peter 1:3-8

Where to take it

❓ Before his death, Caesar says, "When a man sees his end, he wants to know there was some purpose to his life. How will the world speak my name in years to come?" Do you agree with Caesar's observation? Why or why not?

❓ Where might people look to find their purpose?

❓ Describe *your* purpose in life.

❓ Maximus received the highest compliment when Caesar denounced his own son and asked him to lead Rome. Describe a situation where you were asked to do something or received a tribute that honored and humbled you.

❓ In the second clip Commodus recites two sets of virtues to his father: wisdom, justice, fortitude, and temperance versus ambition, resourcefulness, courage, and devotion. Explain why you agree or disagree that both lists contain virtues a person should strive for in life.

❓ How does God view the second set of virtues that Commodus claimed to possess? (Start with James 3:13-18 as it relates to ambition, then see what other verses you can find to answer this question.)

❓ Read Galatians 5:22-26; 1 Peter 5:2-9; and 2 Peter 1:3-8. How do the character traits listed in these passages compare with the virtues Commodus mentioned?

❓ Read Jeremiah 29:11-14; 1 Corinthians 9:24-27; and 1 Peter 1:3-7. What do these passages tell you about a Christian's inheritance from the Lord? What would Commodus think about this type of inheritance? Explain why this eternal inheritance is or isn't valuable to you.

The Green Mile

The movie drama, R

Based on a Stephen King novel, *The Green Mile* takes place in a prison where the guards and inmates have nicknamed death row "The Green Mile" because of the dark green linoleum tiles leading to the execution room. Paul Edgecomb (Tom Hanks) is the head guard. He befriends a new inmate, John Coffey (Michael Clarke Duncan), who was sentenced to die for the murder of two young girls. During John's incarceration, Paul and the other guards discover something special about this gentle giant.

This clip (just under 4 minutes)

This clip is on the second videotape.

▶ **Start** / 0:43:30 / John Coffey is sleeping on a cot as the cell door opens.

⏹ **Stop** / 0:47:16 / "Yes, John, I think I can."

A few days before John's execution, Paul asks for his last requests. John says meatloaf and mashed potatoes would be nice for dinner, but otherwise he doesn't need anything special. Paul admits he's not sure what he'll say on Judgment Day when God wants to know why he executed John. He asks, "What am I going to say? That it was my job?" The convict assures Paul that his execution will be a kindness. He just wants his life of loneliness and pain to be over.

By the Book

Job 9; Matthew 7:21-23; 12:36-37; 18:1-6; 19:14; 2 Timothy 2:19; 4:7-8

Where to take it

- This clip refers to "true miracles." Explain why you do or don't believe there are true miracles in the world today.

- To what do you attribute John's quiet and humble acceptance of his death sentence and pending execution? Is it faith? Is he just guilty? Would "God's true miracle" murder two children?

- Read Job 9. John Coffey could have written these words on death row. Using this passage, list the similarities and differences between Job's and John's circumstances.

- What does it mean to have a childlike faith? What is promised to those who have faith like a child? (See Matthew 18:1-6 and 19:14.) Is your faith in the Lord this great?

- What will happen on Judgment Day? Read Matthew 7:21-23; 12:36-37; 2 Timothy 2:19; and 2 Timothy 4:7-8 for some ideas.

- John talks about how the pain in the world makes him tired, restless, and burdened. Describe a time when you felt so bad for someone or something that it made you feel sick or heavy hearted. How can we care for the burdens of others without being overwhelmed by them?

- When you look back at the end of your life and think about your hopes and dreams, what is one thing you don't want to look back and wish you had done?

Holy Man

Trailer

What do you feel most passionate about?

The movie comedy/drama, PG

Miami's Good Buy Shopping Network is almost broke, so the new owner (Robert Loggia) demands that Ricky Hayman (Jeff Goldblum) increase the company's sales in just two weeks. Nothing Ricky tries increases their profits until he meets "G" (Eddie Murphy) along the side of the road. After witnessing G's positive effect on others, Ricky makes him an on-air spokesperson. G spins spiritual applications around the company's odd product inventory and Good Buy's sales and ratings soar.

This clip (about 2 minutes)

- ▶ **Start** / 1:01:38 / "Okay, okay. Here's the teleprompter...when the red light goes on..."

- ■ **Stop** / 1:03:51 / "Give in ...and take the journey."

G goes on the air to sell a starfish necklace. Ricky starts to sweat when G stops reading the cue cards and tells a story about thousands of starfish that washed up on the beach. He compares people who've lost their way to the beached starfish, and the little girl who tried to save the creatures to the feeling of connectedness that everyone needs in their life. G teaches his audience that making a difference in even one person's life is a big deal.

By the Book

Psalm 119:176; Ecclesiastes 4:9-12; Luke 15:3-7

Where to take it

② When you hear the starfish story, what emotions does it stir in you? How does the story relate to your life?

② Describe someone who made a significant difference in your life and what she did.

② What could you do—once or on a regular basis—to make a difference in someone else's life? List some ideas.

② Read Luke 15:3-7. If you were one of the 99 sheep, how might you feel to be left behind for the sake of the one? If you were the lost sheep, how might you feel to know the shepherd left the other 99 to come rescue you? How are you like that lost sheep?

② The Holy Man says, "That's the only time you're ever alive really, is when you're connecting." What does he mean? Describe times in your life when you feel the most alive.

② G also says, "Let go...give in...and take the journey." What kinds of things do people hold onto that keep them from giving the spiritual aspects of their lives priority? What do you need to let go of, so you can continue your spiritual journey with the Lord unhindered?

Trailer

Which is stronger—hate or love?

The movie drama, R

Denzel Washington plays Rubin "Hurricane" Carter, a boxer convicted of murder at the height of his career. While serving consecutive life terms in prison, Rubin's appeals are repeatedly denied, and his hope is slowly dying. When young Lesra Martin (Vicellous Reon Shannon) reads Carter's book, *The Sixteenth Round*, he begins writing letters to Rubin. Lesra knows he can't free Rubin alone, so he enlists the help of three Canadian activists. Together they set out to prove Rubin's innocence despite the obstacles that continue to erode his hope for freedom and restitution.

This clip (just under 2 minutes)

- ▶ **Start** / 1:36:00 / Rubin walks past a man bench pressing.

- ■ **Stop** / 1:37:50 / "Okay...okay."

Terry (John Hannah) asks Rubin to look out the window while they're talking on the phone. When he does, Rubin sees a room light flashing on and off in a building across the way, and the silhouettes of three people jumping up and down. Terry explains that they've moved closer in order to work on Rubin's appeal full time. Just when he'd almost given up hope, Rubin is reminded that he's not fighting this battle alone.

By the Book

2 Samuel 22:29-37; Proverbs 18:24; Matthew 5:14-16; John 15:12-13; Romans 12:9-19; 1 John 2:9-11

Where to take it

- Describe a time when you felt imprisoned and friends came along and helped you through it.

- Who could use some reassurance that you'll stick by them no matter what happens in his life? Who can you count on to be there for you until the very end?

- John 15:12-13 talks about a friendship so great that a person is willing to lay down his life for another. Think about the people in your life. Who would you willingly die for? Who in your life might be willing to die for you?

- Read 2 Samuel 22:29-37; Matthew 5:14-16 (if possible, read this one from *The Message*); Romans 12:9-19; and 1 John 2:9-11. List some ways you can be a light to a friend.

- On a scale of one (the light bulb is off) to five (as bright as the sun), rate how brightly your light shines in other people's lives. What can you do to shine brighter?

Independence Day

Trailer

Which is more important to you—freedom on earth or freedom in Christ?

The movie action/science fiction, PG-13

Extraterrestrial beings are attacking Earth, and no one knows why. These aliens know what they're doing, destroying the largest and most influential cities around the globe first. Panic quickly becomes chaos as these cities' populations attempt a mass evacuation for safety. Meanwhile, the world's military forces have been reduced to a ragtag group of soldiers who must unite and figure out a way to save the planet from total domination.

This clip (just under 2 minutes)

▶ **Start** / 1:47:10 / "Major, can I borrow that?"

⏹ **Stop** / 1:49:00 / The crowd cheers and applauds.

Freedom fighters gather to prepare for a counterattack. The president of the United States (Bill Pullman) delivers a battle cry to the soldiers before they head off to war on the Fourth of July. He rallies the troops and asks them to think about what they're fighting for—freedom from annihilation, their right to live, and their futures. After this war is over, July 4th will no longer be an American holiday. The whole world will celebrate Independence Day.

By the Book

Psalm 91:9-12; Matthew 13:24-30, 36-43; Romans 5:6-11; 6:19-23; Galatians 5:1, 13-14, 19-26; Revelation 19:11-16

Where to take it

⟨?⟩ The president mentions putting aside petty differences to fight for one cause. What petty differences could he be referring to? List some current world events that illustrate differences that exist between our country and other nations or between ethnic groups.

⟨?⟩ What freedoms do we enjoy in our country that people in other countries do not? In what ways are we not free? What groups of people living in this country might say they aren't free? Why do they think so?

⟨?⟩ Read Psalm 91:9-12; Matthew 13:24-30, 36-43; and any other passages you can find that refer to angels or demons at work. Summarize your understanding of these verses.

⟨?⟩ Describe a time in your life—or a friends' life or a public event—when spiritual forces might have been influencing the activity.

⟨?⟩ What character traits or mental images come to mind when you think about Jesus? Read the description of Jesus in Revelation 19:11-16. How does this picture of Jesus compare with the images you just listed? Why don't most people usually think of Jesus in this way?

⟨?⟩ Read Romans 5:6-11; 6:19-23; and Galatians 5:1, 13-14, 19-26. What does it mean to have freedom in Christ? How do you experience this freedom? What can you do to shine brighter?

Instinct **Trailer**

How do you feel about people who think the world revolves around them?

The movie drama/thriller, R

Dr. Ethan Powell (Anthony Hopkins) is an anthropologist who becomes consumed with the mountain gorillas of Rwanda and decides to live among them. When a search party later finds Ethan and shoots a gorilla, he flies into a murderous rage and kills two people. Dr. Theo Calder (Cuba Gooding Jr.) meets Ethan in a maximum-security facility in the States. However, the once distinguished scientist reacts more like a frightened animal than a human being. As he gains the prisoner's trust, Theo learns some things about himself as well.

This clip (just under 3 minutes)

▶ **Start** / 1:13:50 / Theo enters Ethan's jail cell.

⏹ **Stop** / 1:16:15 / A close-up shot of Theo's face.

Theo comes to the prison after Ethan has drawn an intricate map of the world on the walls of his cell. Theo starts to ask questions and receives a lesson on "the true history" of mankind and how it evolved. Ethan describes how tribal societies had their place in the world, yet they shared it. Then Ethan says, "We changed all that." Theo asks what can be done to change the past.

By the Book

Psalm 22:27-28; 1 Peter 1:22-2:3, 11-17; 2 Peter 1:3-8

Where to take it

(?) What does Ethan mean when he says, "We have only one thing to give up—our dominion. We don't own the world."

(?) If we don't own the world, who does (see Psalm 22:27-28)?

(?) Why is it hard for humans to give up control or dominion? (*Dominion* means "supreme authority or absolute ownership.")

(?) Read 1 Peter 1:22-2:3, 11-17 and 2 Peter 1:3-8. Describe the ways these verses speak against seeking domination. How do they suggest we live instead?

(?) Where's the line, if any, between the scientific pursuit of knowledge and playing God?

(?) What are the areas, if any, that science should not enter?

(?) Now that the world's population is over six billion people, what can you do to avoid feeling insignificant?

(?) In what ways can a single individual make a difference? What contribution do you hope to make in this world?

I.Q.

Trailer

Do cheaters ever prosper?

The movie — comedy/romance, PG

Ed Walters (Tim Robbins) is a simple auto mechanic who falls in love with Catherine (Meg Ryan), the niece of Albert Einstein (Walter Matthau). However, Catherine is attracted to a highly intelligent but smug Princeton man named James Moreland (Stephen Fry). Uncle Albert believes that Ed and Catherine were made for each another, so he conjures up a scheme to make Ed look smarter. And Ed needs all the help he can get as he tries to win Catherine's heart.

This clip — (about 3 minutes)

- ▶ **Start** / 0:57:32 / "Yes, uh, quite impressive. Now let's move on to phase two."

- ■ **Stop** / 1:00:41 / "I'm done. Is that it?"

James doesn't believe that Ed is a scientific genius. To prove his theory, and humiliate Ed in the process, James invites him to perform some psychological tasks and answer some questions about "general knowledge" in front of a room full of university professors and reporters. Ed does well in the first round, but he doesn't know a single answer on the multiple-choice quiz—until Uncle Albert and his buddies come to the rescue.

cheating, deception,
the end justifying the means, integrity

By the Book

Leviticus 19:1-2, 11; Proverbs 10:9; 11:3; Ephesians 4:22-25;
Titus 2:6-8; 1 Peter 2:1

Where to take it

● When might it be okay to cheat? Talk about that.

● Without naming names, describe a situation when you witnessed someone cheating. Why did you—or didn't you—turn them in?

● Describe a situation when you were tempted to cheat. What happened?

● When a person cheats, what are the immediate positive and negative effects?

● How might cheating positively and negatively impact a student's future?

● What impact does a student's cheating have on the other people in the class, including the teacher?

● What does integrity mean? Is it something you can learn? How do people get or use more *integrity* in their lives?

● Name two people you know who live a life of integrity, and explain why you chose them.

The Iron Giant

Trailer

Would you be willing to break the law for someone you loved?

The movie — family/animation/science fiction, PG

Hogarth Hughes (voice of Eli Marienthal) is a nine-year-old boy who dreams about invasions from outer space and fighting off Communist agents. To Hogarth's surprise something better and much bigger drops into a nearby lake and into Hogarth's life—a 50-foot tall robot. Hogarth and the Iron Giant (voice of Vin Diesel) become instant friends. However, when government agent Mansley (voice of Christopher McDonald) hears about the robot, he wants it terminated.

This clip (just under 4 minutes)

▶ **Start** / 1:13:07 / "Launch the missile now!"

⏹ **Stop** / 1:16:43 / A star shines in the sky.

Agent Mansley just released a nuclear bomb into the earth's atmosphere, leaving the Iron Giant with a difficult decision. Does he stay on Earth and watch his new friend Hogarth die? Or should he leap into space and stop the bomb, knowing he will die in the process? The robot looks at the people with compassion. Will he make the ultimate sacrifice so mankind may live?

By the Book

John 3:16; 15:9-17; Romans 6:22-23; Titus 2:11-14

Where to take it

🌀 Describe a time when you gave something up for the sake of a friendship. In the end was saving the friendship worth the sacrifice you made? Why or why not?

🌀 Read John 15:9-17. What word is repeated throughout the passage? What does it mean to "lay down your life for a friend"?

🌀 Describe a time when you put yourself on the line for someone else. What was the outcome for each of you?

🌀 A friend asks you, "How can a loving God allow all the pain and suffering in the world?" How would you respond?

Trailer

Is it ever okay to tell a lie?

The movie comedy/drama, PG-13

Set during the Nazi occupation of Poland during World War 2, *Jakob the Liar* tells the story of a Polish Jew (Robin Williams) who uses his imagination to bring hope to his friends in the ghetto. One day Jakob illegally hears information broadcast through a Nazi soldier's radio about the advancement of the Russian army. He shares what he heard with his friends but pretends he heard it on his own secret radio. Once Jakob realizes that his phony broadcasts boost morale in the Jewish community, he starts to make up and share more information about the imminent defeat of the Nazis.

This clip [4 minutes]

▶ **Start** / 1:07:25 / "You sit here, eh."

⏹ **Stop** / 1:11:25 / Jakob and Lina dance in the basement.

Jakob broadcasts a report about Russian advancements for Lina (Hannah Taylor-Gordon), a girl he's cared for since she lost her parents. Even though Jakob struggles morally with his deceit, he cannot escape how happy the radio stories make his friends and neighbors, just as he can't escape the hope that his phony radio gives little Lina.

By the Book

1 Chronicles 29:17; Psalm 26:2-3; Jeremiah 17:9-10; 1 Corinthians 4:5;
Philippians 1:18

Where to take it

In this scene did Jakob lie to Lina or for Lina? What's the difference
between these two phrases? Is what he did a sin?

Read Philippians 1:18. How might
this verse apply to the scene?

How often do you lie during a
day, including little white lies?

Is it possible to live your life
without lying at all? Explain your
opinion.

When might it be okay to lie?
Talk about that.

POP
CORN

Jurassic Park

Trailer

Have you ever felt trapped by the sins of your past?

The movie — horror/action/thriller/adventure/science fiction, PG-13

An eccentric millionaire named John Hammond (Richard Attenborough) invites Dr. Alan Grant (Sam Neill) and Dr. Ellie Sattler (Laura Dern) to preview his new Jurassic amusement park full of genetically cloned prehistoric beasts. The two scientists are amazed at how the dinosaurs peacefully coexist with the humans. That is until one of Mr. Hammond's guests damages the security system and tries to take some frozen dinosaur embryos as souvenirs. Once the island habitat is altered and the dinosaurs are free to wander where they please, they leave a wake of destruction across the island.

This clip (just under 3 minutes)

▶ **Start** / 1:15:42 / "Tim?"

⏹ **Stop** / 1:18:07 / "At least you're out of the tree."

In this scene Mr. Hammond's grandson Tim (Joseph Mazzello) gets stuck in a tour car that has been thrust high atop some trees. Alan attempts to rescue him, but Tim is too scared to move. Alan knows the only way they'll both live is if the boy takes a chance and gets out of the car. He hopes Tim takes that chance soon before the branch breaks and they both fall to their doom.

By the Book

2 Chronicles 20:9; Psalm 103:8-14; Ezekiel 18:21-23; James 1:2-4, 12;
1 John 1:9

Where to take it

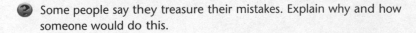

● Why is change so hard for many people? What can those people do to make change easier on themselves? What can you do so the next time change occurs you'll embrace it instead of resist it?

● Describe a time when you had to deal with a mistake from your past.

● Explain why it's easy or hard for you to get over your mistakes. How could dwelling too much on the past hurt you in the present?

● Read Psalm 103:8-14; Ezekiel 18:21-23; and 1 John 1:9. Summarize what these verses teach about forgiveness and how God deals with sin. Does this seem consistent with your experience? Talk about that.

● Read 2 Chronicles 20:9 and then James 1:2-4, 12. Describe why God doesn't always answer our prayers by saving us from change or sparing us from making mistakes in our lives. What purpose do mistakes serve?

● Some people say they treasure their mistakes. Explain why and how someone would do this.

Keeping the Faith

Trailer

What is God calling you to do or be in this world?

The movie drama/comedy/romance, PG-13

Father Brian Finn (Edward Norton) and Rabbi Jacob Schram (Ben Stiller) have been best friends since their youth. When their childhood pal Anna (Jenna Elfman) returns to New York, both men are amazed that her beauty and success haven't spoiled her fun-loving and compassionate nature. Both Brian and Jacob consider dating Anna, but they must also consider the impact this romantic relationship would have on their ministries and their friendship.

This clip (about 2 minutes)

▶ **Start** / 1:35:39 / Father Havel lights a cigar.

⏹ **Stop** / 1:37:55 / "God will give you your answer."

Brian is wrestling with thoughts of giving up the priesthood to pursue a life with Anna. He wants to know what he should do, and he wants to know right now. Father Havel (Milos Forman) shares how he almost gave up his calling for the love of a woman. Then he tells the young priest that when you're called to do something in life, you may have to recommit yourself to that calling occasionally. As for discovering some quick answers, Father Havel reminds Brian that only God has the answer and that it will come in his timing.

By the Book

Romans 8:28; 1 Corinthians 1:26–2:5; Ephesians 4:1; 2 Peter 1:10-11

Where to take it

● What does Father Havel mean when he talks about regularly recommitting yourself to your calling?

● Read Ephesians 4:1 and 2 Peter 1:10-11. What does God mean in these verses by our "calling"?

● Does God provide the answers to our problems, let us figure out the answers on our own, or something in between? Explain your thinking.

● Read Romans 8:28. Explain what this verse means. Explain what it doesn't mean.

The Matrix

Trailer

Are you willing to live life outside your comfort zone?

The movie   action/thriller/science fiction, R

Virtual reality is more than just a game—it's a way to imprison you. Thomas Anderson (Keanu Reeves) is a computer whiz working for a software company and a hacker on the side. In the year 2070 Thomas meets Morpheous (Laurence Fishburne) and learns that the life he knows isn't real. Morpheous reveals the secret of the Matrix—an imaginary world based on 20th-century Earth where humans' minds live while their bodies are used as batteries by a sinister artificial intelligence system.

This clip (about 4 minutes)

▶ **Start** / 0:25:23 / "This is it...let me give you one piece of advice...be honest...he knows more than you can possibly imagine."

⏹ **Stop** / 0:29:40 / "Follow me."

Thomas must decide whether or not to accept the truth and all that comes with it. Morpheus asks him to choose between two pills—red or blue. The blue pill will allow him to return to the life he's accustomed to, but the red pill will give him the ability to see everything as it truly is and pursue a brand new life full of adventure. Will Thomas choose the deadened comfort of his old life or an abundant new life?

By the Book

John 15:18-19; Romans 12:1-2; 1 Corinthians 3:18-20; 2 Corinthians 10:3-4; James 4:4; 1 Peter 2:11-17; 1 John 2:15-17

Where to take it

- Imagine that God has a red pill. If you were to take it, describe what you expect the new world—the kingdom of God—to be like. Does it exist on Earth or only in heaven? If it's on Earth, where can people find it?

- If you were to use any part of the Bible to convince someone to choose the kingdom of God, what aspects of Christianity would you use to persuade them? What ideas might scare them off?

- A common theme in Scripture is the idea of not acting or thinking like the world around you. On a scale of one (as easy as taking Skittles from a baby) to 100 (as hard as getting gum out of frizzy hair), rate how easy it is for you to resist peer pressure (make your own choices instead of doing what your friends are doing, going against popular culture, etc). Explain how you make your decisions.

- Describe a time when you didn't follow the crowd. Did people treat you differently after that?

- Thomas declares that he doesn't believe in fate because he doesn't like the idea of not being in control of his life. Why is it hard for some people to give up control? How much control does a person have to give up to be a follower of God? Explain why giving up control is hard or easy for you to do.

Meet Joe Black

Trailer

Do you find it easy or difficult to speak the truth?

The movie   fantasy/romance/drama, PG-13

The Angel of Death is bored. Lately he's been closely observing William Parrish (Anthony Hopkins), whose lifestyle intrigues him. Just before Bill's 65th birthday, Death delivers a proposal to the wealthy businessman. If Bill agrees to serve as Death's guide, he'll get more time on earth. Should Bill tell anyone who Death is, then the deal is off—no more second chances. Bill adds his own proviso to their contract: Death cannot take anyone else in his family during this trip.

This clip   (just under 2 minutes)

The clip is taken from the first videotape. Be prepared to stop the video immediately—this scene ends unexpectedly and shows a car hitting a man in the street.

▶ **Start** / 0:20:29 / Oh boy. Okay, now I gotta go...so..."

⏹ **Stop** / 0:22:00 / Scene fades from busy intersection.

A young man (Brad Pitt) meets Bill's daughter Susan (Claire Forlani) in a coffee shop. The scene picks up as they're parting on the sidewalk. While neither one is brave enough to say what they're really thinking, it's obvious they'd like to spend more time together—it's written all over their faces. However, whenever Susan or her mystery man turns around, the other one is walking in the opposite direction.

By the Book

Exodus 4:10-13; Psalm 15:1-2; Romans 8:26-27; Ephesians 4:22-25; 5:15-17

Where to take it

- People spend too much time telling others what they want to hear instead of sharing how they really feel. Explain why you agree or disagree with this statement.

- Describe a time when you decided not to tell someone the truth about your feelings. What was the outcome? Do you regret your decision? If you had it to do over, would you do things differently?

- On a scale from one (I just can't get the words out) to 10 (I'm a natural born communicator), how good are you at sharing your emotions and communicating your feelings with others?

- On a scale of one (it's like talking to a brick wall!) to 10 (we hear more than we ever wanted to know!), where would your friends rank you regarding your vulnerability and communication skills? Where would your family rank you? If their rankings are different from yours, explain why they differ.

- Where do you think God would rank you? How often do you spend time talking with him? During your prayer times are you brutally honest with God about your feelings? If not, explain why you struggle to be honest with him.

- Read Romans 8:26-27. Rewrite the verse in your own words. Talk about what the verses mean.

The Messenger: The Story of Joan of Arc

Trailer

Do you find it easy or difficult to speak the truth?

The movie drama/war, R

France is embroiled in The Hundred Years' War with England, and young Jeanne d'Aragon (Milla Jovovich) hears the voice of God telling her to lead the French army into battle and defend their land against the British. Jeanne is dubbed "Joan of Arc," and she bravely guides her army in a holy battle.

This clip (about 1 minute)

▶ **Start** / 1:49:14 / "Who are you?"

■ **Stop** / 1:50:25 / Ends with Joan of Arc receiving several slaps to the face.

Joan is being held captive by the British when Satan (Dustin Hoffman) pays her a visit. When Joan asks Satan about his identity, he tries to confuse her by changing his appearance to resemble the young boy and later the young man she saw in her visions when God confirmed that he had chosen her for a special purpose. Once Joan rebukes Satan, he tries a new tactic where he mentally and spiritually tries to beat Joan down by questioning her ability to judge between good and evil and mocking her for thinking God needs her help. Despite her state of physical weakness, Joan holds on to what she knows is true and resists Satan's lies.

By the Book

Deuteronomy 18:17-22; Job 1:6-12; Mark 16:14-16; Acts 26:12-18; 2 Corinthians 2:10-11; Revelation 12:7-12

Where to take it

- ❓ What's the difference between good and evil? Is the difference always clear? Why or why not?

- ❓ Read Job 1:6-12; 2 Corinthians 2:10-11; and Revelation 12:7-12. What are some things about Satan that we need to be aware of? What other verses describe Satan besides the ones mentioned here?

- ❓ Describe a time when you experienced false guilt or negative feelings toward God—a time when you eventually realized that Satan was falsely accusing you or lying in your ear so you would neglect your relationship with God. How did you break free? Did you finally figure it out on your own? Did God tap you on the shoulder? Did a friend or relative help you see what was going on?

- ❓ What's our best defense against Satan's tricks? What can we do to deflect his spiritual attacks and stay focused on the Lord? What Bible verses support your thoughts?

- ❓ Satan asks Joan, "How can you possibly imagine that God, the creator of heaven and earth, the source of all life, could possibly need *you*?" Does God *need* us? Talk about that. What does God need us—or simply use our help—for? Make a list.

- ❓ Are prophets different from regular people? If so, how? (Read Deuteronomy 18:17-22 and Acts 26:12-18 for some ideas.)

Mission: Impossible 2

Trailer

Do you believe in love at first sight?

The movie
action/adventure/mystery/
thriller, PG-13

Ethan Hunt (Tom Cruise) is an operative for the Impossible Missions
Force (IMF), a top-secret government agency. His mission—should
he choose to accept it—is to track down a former IMF agent gone
bad, Sean Ambrose (Dougray Scott). Sean stole a sample of
Chimera, a deadly synthetic virus with the capacity to terminate a
large portion of the world's population, and he plans to sell it to the
highest bidder. Ethan is instructed to approach Sean's ex-girlfriend
Nyah (Thandie Newton) and ask her to help IMF by winning back
Sean's confidence and retrieving the Chimera so it can't harm
anyone. But first Ethan has to find her.

This clip (about 1 minute)

▶ **Start** / 0:11:00 / Ethan puts a glass on a
tray.

⏹ **Stop** / 0:12:17 / Ethan looks around the
room for Nyah.

Ethan tracks down Nyah at a wealthy entrepreneur's party. The two
spot each other across the room and neither one is willing to look
away first. As Flamenco dancers, with their colorful costumes and
rhythmic movements, entertain the party guests, Ethan and Nyah do
a dance of their own.

By the Book

Matthew 5:28; Romans 13:13-14; Ephesians 4:18-19; 5:3-7;
Colossians 3:1-5

Where to take it

- How realistic do you generally find the portrayal of love in the movies?

- If you believe it's unrealistic, why do people find that misrepresentation of love so appealing?

- Do movies generally have too much sex, not enough sex, or an appropriate amount for the stories they tell? Why do you think so?

- Some say that all romantic relationships start with physical attraction. Explain why you agree or disagree with that opinion.

- What are the problems with a guy and a girl having a purely physical relationship?

Mr. Mom

Trailer

What security blankets do you hold onto in life?

The movie comedy/drama, PG

Jack Butler (Michael Keaton) has lost his job. After his fruitless search for new employment, his wife Caroline (Terri Garr) takes a job at an ad agency, leaving Jack to adjust to the pioneer role of stay-at-home dad. At first he resents the role reversal, feeling out of place with the neighborhood moms and being mocked by the men. Chaos reigns around the house until Jack stops feeling sorry for himself and starts tackling the most important job he'll ever have.

This clip (about 2 minutes)

▶ **Start** / 0:59:35 / Kenny is sitting on the floor of his room.

⏹ **Stop** / 1:01:48 / "You had to do it."

Kenny (Taliesin Jaffe), Jack's middle child, has carried a blanket around since he was a baby. His "wubby" helps him feel safe. However Kenny isn't a baby any more, and the blanket has seen better days. Jack believes it's time for Kenny to let go of his security blanket and take some chances. Kenny takes a big step when he reluctantly trusts his dad and lets go of a huge part of his childhood.

By the Book

Psalm 23; 34:4; Isaiah 40:17-20, 28-31; 41:10-13; Habakkuk 2:18-20; 1 John 4:16-18

Where to take it

🌀 What are some security blankets that teens and adults hold onto? Which ones are good? Which ones aren't? What are some good and bad aspects about using these for comfort?

🌀 Think about a security blanket in your life—your wubby. Explain why it's a positive or negative influence. What would it take for you to let go of it?

🌀 Think about your parents. What are their security blankets? Why do they find security there?

🌀 List some benefits and consequences of letting go of what gives you comfort.

🌀 Read Psalm 23; Psalm 34:4; Isaiah 41:10-13; and 1 John 4:16-18. How does your wubby compare to the comfort and security that God offers?

🌀 The Bible uses the term *idol*. What do idols have to do with security blankets? (See Isaiah 40:17-20, 28-31 and Habakkuk 2:18-20.)

🌀 List some modern interests, items, or even people that are made into idols today.

🌀 Could a wubby become an idol? Explain.

Mr. Smith Goes to Washington

Trailer

Have you ever fought for a lost cause?

The movie   drama, NR

Jefferson Smith (James Stewart) was unexpectedly appointed junior senator. At first the other senators tease Jeff about his lack of political qualifications, but this only spurs him on to figure out how the legislative system works and what part he plays. Wanting to give something back to the boys in his state, Jeff proposes a bill to create a national boys' camp. However it's met with great opposition when it's revealed that the suggested building site is the same location where a powerful senior senator has plans to build a dam.

This clip   (about 6 minutes)

▶ **Start** / 2:00:35 / "Senator Smith has now talked for 23 hours and 16 minutes."

⏹ **Stop** / 2:07:00 / Senator Smith collapses on the floor.

Jeff pleads with his colleagues, asking them to give American boys a place to go where they can learn how to become tomorrow's leaders. He agrees to yield the floor for a question from Senator Paine (Claude Raines) who reveals that people from their home state have sent 50,000 telegrams asking Jeff to give up. Surprised but undaunted, Jeff reminds the older senator of something the senator once said to Jeff—lost causes are the only ones worth fighting for.

By the Book

Luke 10:27; Romans 12:1-2; 1 Timothy 4:15; Hebrews 12:1; James 1:27; 1 Peter 3:8-9, 13-14

Where to take it

- Senator Smith says that lost causes are worth fighting for because of one rule: love thy neighbor. (See Luke 10:27.) Why do you believe it is or isn't possible to always follow the Golden Rule today?

- Describe someone whose beliefs or commitment to her beliefs annoys or troubles you. What is commendable and what is harmful about the amount of passion she shows in support of her beliefs?

- Describe a lost cause you fought for when no one else seemed to care. What was the outcome?

- For nearly 24 hours Mr. Smith fought for what he believed in until he was hoarse and eventually collapsed. Under what conditions would you dedicate a similar amount of time and energy to something—even if you knew it might not work?

- Read Romans 12:1-2; 1 Timothy 4:15; Hebrews 12:1; James 1:27; and 1 Peter 3:8-9, 13-14. In what ways could these verses encourage you to keep fighting for what you believe? What promises are made to those who don't give up?

Mulan Trailer

What boosts your self-confidence?

The movie family/animation, G

In the time that this story takes place, Chinese women brought their families honor by marrying well and having sons. However, Mulan (voice of Ming-Na) is not a typical Chinese girl. When Mulan's father is called to join the army and fight the Huns, she believes he won't survive another war. So Mulan pretends to be his son and enlists to fight in her father's place. If the truth is discovered, there will be ultimate dishonor for her father and death for Mulan.

This clip (about 2 minutes)

▶ **Start** / 1:01:58 / "I was this close...this close."

⏹ **Stop** / 1:04:08 / "I promise."

After her regiment abandons her in the mountains, Mulan admits she joined the army with less than honorable intentions. She really wanted to prove that she could do something right and that her life is worthwhile, but she ended up feeling like a bigger failure than before. Mushu (voice of Eddie Murphy) tries to offer a little comfort by confessing that he's also a fraud. Regardless of their intentions, it's time to go home and face the consequences—and Mulan's father. Mushu promises they'll do so together.

By the Book

Psalm 34:17-18; Proverbs 3:21-26; Luke 15:11-24; Hebrews 12:7-11; Revelation 3:19

Where to take it

● Before this scene began, Mulan's bravery stopped the Huns and saved her commander's life. Yet Mulan says she sees nothing when she looks at her reflection. How can Mulan let one mistake negate all the good she's done since joining the army? Can you relate to her way of thinking? If it's true for you, explain why you forget all of the good stuff about yourself when you're feeling low.

● Mulan isn't looking forward to facing her father. On a scale of two (I can talk about anything at any time) to nine (no one understands me!) rate how easy or difficult it is for you to talk with your parents when you're feeling down.

● Using the same scale, rate how easy or difficult it is for you to talk to God when you're blue.

● Now rate yourself in terms of talking to your friends in the same situation. If there's a significant difference between the three ratings, explain why.

● Who are the people you talk to the most when you're feeling down. Make a list of ways they try to cheer you up or to comfort you. Which ways work best for you?

● Hebrews 12:7-11 tells how God proves his love for us through discipline. Name some ways that discipline can serve as proof of love.

● Read the parable of the lost son in Luke 15:11-24. How might this story encourage Mulan as she heads home? What does it say to you about talking with your parents about your mistakes? How does this parable—and Psalm 34:17-18— encourage you to talk to God?

117

The Mummy

Trailer

Whose life plan are you following?

The movie — adventure/action/horror, PG-13

Over 3,000 years ago, Im-Ho-Tep (Arnold Vosloo) was a high priest to Pharaoh Seti (Aharon Ipalé) and responsible for preparing the dead for their journey into the next life. Im-Ho-Tep fell in love with the Pharaoh's misstress, Anck-Su-Namun (Patricia Velazquez) and killed Pharaoh in order to have Anck-Su-Namun all to himself. The priest was caught and buried alive in a horrific tomb. Now a band of renegades, led by Rick O'Connell (Brendan Fraser), stumbles onto the unknown burial site and accidentally releases the mummy of Im-Ho-Tep, who is hungry to regain what should have been his thousands of years before.

This clip (just under 2 minutes)

- ▶ **Start** / 1:06:42 / Beni runs inside the tomb holding a torch and a gun.

- ■ **Stop** / 1:08:12 / "My prince!"

Beni (Kevin J. O'Connor) hopes to get away with all the valuables he can carry, but staying alive is his main objective. Soon he comes face to face with the mummy and desperately shows him several religious symbols that he wears around his neck for protection. As the mummy continues to advance, Beni realizes there is no escape and agrees to do the mummy's evil bidding in exchange for his life—but at what price?

By the Book

Matthew 4:1-11; 6:19-21, 24; 16:24-27; 25:31-46; 1 Timothy 6:6-13

Where to take it

- Explain why you do or don't believe in charms and magic.

- What is the most tempting thing about doing evil? What is the scariest thing about it?

- Read Matthew 4:1-11. What was the main thing Jesus did to resist Satan's temptations? What Scripture passages can you think of that could have stopped the mummy in his tracks if Beni had used them?

- Do you ever use the Bible to help you resist temptation? If so, describe a time when you did and share the outcome.

- When do people usually call on God? Describe a situation when you cried out for God's help. What happened?

- What is the world's plan or expectation for living a full life? Generally speaking, how are people rewarded for following this plan?

- Read Matthew 6:19-21, 24; 16:24-27; 25:31-46; and 1 Timothy 6:6-13. Now describe God's plan for living a full life. How are people rewarded when they follow God's plan instead of the world's?

- What's the most important thing you can do with the life you've been given?

Trailer

What past events have shaped your character today?

The movie drama/family, PG

Willie Morris (Frankie Muniz) has a few strikes against him. His dad came home from the war more stern and overbearing than when he left. His mother is not like a typical housewife. And Willie is an only child—an oddity in the 1940s. He doesn't have friends his own age and can't think of a single person to invite to his birthday party. But all of that ceases to matter when Willie receives a Jack Russell terrier. With Skip's help, Willie gains self-confidence and even befriends the neighborhood bullies who used to torment him.

This clip (just under 4 minutes)

- ▶ **Start** / 1:23:45 / Willie cries over his dog Skip as he lies on an operating table.
- ■ **Stop** / 1:27:22 / "And surely the most lasting."

Willie is by Skip's side all night after surgery. He begs the dog not to leave him, lists the ways Skip has helped him, then admits he'll never have another friend like him. Looking back, a grown-up Willie (Harry Connick Jr.) admits he became a young man the day he nearly lost Skip and credits the dog's friendship for his successes in school and his career, knowing that a life without Skip wouldn't have been the same.

By the Book

Psalm 119:9-16; Proverbs 20:29; Ecclesiastes 4:9-12; 11:9–12:5; 1 Timothy 5:1-8; 1 Peter 5:5-8

Where to take it

- Describe a lesson you learned when you were younger, including how you came to learn that lesson and how it has influenced the kind of person you are today.

- What does Psalm 119:9-16 teach young Christians about how to live? Do you strive to accomplish any of the suggestions made in this passage? If so, which ones?

- Read and explain Proverbs 20:29. How are older people treated in America? How does this compare to the rest of the world? How do you treat older people when you see them?

- Read 1 Timothy 5:1-8 and 1 Peter 5:5-8. How does the Bible say we should treat people who are older?

- Read Ecclesiastes 11:9–12:5. What types of word pictures are used in this section? What do they mean? (Hint: grinders refers to teeth.) Now that you're aware of these metaphors, talk about what this passage means.

- Willie says, "Loyalty and love are the best things of all and surely the most lasting." Do you agree or disagree? Either explain why you agree, or share what you believe will last longer than love and loyalty and why you believe it's true.

- Read Ecclesiastes 4:9-12. This passage talks about a friendship between two, so what is verse 12 referring to when it says "a cord of three strands"?

- Which of your friendships are stronger—the ones with Christians or the ones with non-Christians? Explain why this is true in your situation. Which friendships have the most positive influence on you? Explain.

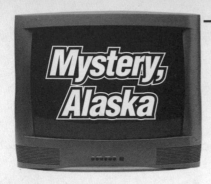

Mystery, Alaska

Trailer

When was the last time you paid someone a compliment?

The movie — comedy, R

The residents of Mystery, Alaska, are obsessed with hockey. In fact once a week everyone turns out for the regular Saturday game. As a publicity stunt, the National Hockey League plans to send the New York Rangers to play against the rag-tag Alaskan team. The town borrows money to build an outdoor ice arena, and the game is all anyone talks about. However, the Rangers keep changing their minds about playing, which sends the town into great upheaval.

This clip (2 minutes)

▶ **Start** / 1:17:50 / John is sitting at the kitchen table.

⏹ **Stop** / 1:19:50 / Donna looks at the paper.

John Biebe (Russell Crowe), Mystery's hockey coach, and his wife Donna (Mary McCormack) have been fighting since her old boyfriend arrived to pitch the idea for the Rangers game. For a tough guy like John, it's difficult to say how he's feeling, so he crosses out all the words in a "Dear Abby" column instead, leaving only the ones that describe his wife and his relationship with her. John's silent yet creative approach sends Donna an overdue message of love and affection—loud and clear.

By the Book

Proverbs 16:24; 1 Corinthians 7:3-5; 13:4-7; Ephesians 5:21-33; Colossians 3:18-19; Titus 2:4-6; 1 Peter 3:1-4, 7; 4:8

Where to take it

- Read 1 Corinthians 7:3-5; Ephesians 5:21-33; Colossians 3:18-19; Titus 2:4-6; and 1 Peter 3:1-4, 7. Make a list of the ways a husband is supposed to show love to his wife. Now list the ways a wife should show love to her husband.

- Guys, read the list of instructions you just wrote down for the husband. On a scale of one (piece of cake) to 10 (no way!), rate how easy or difficult you think it would be to treat your future wife as these passages suggest. Explain your reasoning.

- Girls, read the list of instructions you wrote down regarding the wife. On a scale of one (it would be my pleasure) to 10 (what does *submit* mean?), rate how easy or difficult you believe it would be to treat your future husband as these passages suggest. Explain why you feel this way.

- Describe a real-life example of these biblical attitudes or behaviors between a husband and wife. What do you imagine this couple's relationship is like on a daily basis?

- Who do you express your love to the most—your parents, your siblings, your friends, or a boyfriend or girlfriend? Explain why they're most often the lucky recipients of your love.

- Describe how you show love to others—by writing a note, making a phone call, listening, giving a gift, or anything else you do.

- Read 1 Corinthians 13:4-7. How is love described? List the attributes of love.

- Which traits of love are the most important? Are any unimportant? Explain your reasoning.

- Read Proverbs 16:24 and 1 Peter 4:8. Think of someone who could use a few words of affirmation right now. What would you like to say to her? What does she need to hear? Commit to share these words with her this week.

123

The Natural

Trailer

In the game of life, are you playing your best or sitting on the bench?

The movie drama, PG

When Roy Hobbs (Robert Redford) was 19, a bullet wound sidetracked his baseball career with the Cubs. Now, 16 years later, he's getting another chance to play professional baseball, this time with the 1939 New York Knights. Coach Pop Fisher (Wilford Brimley) wants this last-place team to go to the World Series before he retires, so he leaves the 35-year-old rookie on the bench for most of the season. When Roy finally gets his chance to play, his first hit is a home run that knocks the cover off the ball, earning him a regular spot in the line-up.

This clip (about 6 minutes)

▶ **Start** / 2:07:19 / "Young John Rhodes strides to the mound."

⏹ **Stop** / 2:13:27 / The scene fades.

It's the most important game of Roy's life—and his last. As he stands ready at the plate, Roy faces a number of obstacles—a terrible pain in his side, an inferior bat, and a pitcher who's younger and faster than he is. Yet Roy is determined to finish strong. He doesn't want to live the rest of his life wondering *what if*?

124

By the Book

Job 1:8–2:10; 42:1-6, 12-17; Romans 5:3-5; 2 Corinthians 4:7-9, 16-18; 1 Timothy 6:11-12; Hebrews 10:35-36; James 5:11

Where to take it

● Describe a time when you missed an opportunity. Explain why it was hard—or easy—for you to move on with your life afterward.

● What characteristics come to mind when you think about people who handle difficult circumstances well?

● What characteristics can prevent a person from dealing with difficulties in a positive or healthy way?

● Read Job 1:8–2:10. How do you describe Job's response to the tragedy in his life? How did his wife respond? How would you respond in this situation?

● Read Job 1:8 again, but this time replace Job's name with your own. (If you're female, also change the pronouns to *her* and *she* and change *man to woman,* so it makes sense when you read it!) How would you feel if the Lord said this about you?

● James 5:11 says Job persevered. What things did he do to survive these terrible circumstances? What was the ultimate result of Job's perseverance? (See Job 42:12-17.) What did Job learn about God through this experience? (See Job 42:1-6.)

● Read Romans 5:3-5; 2 Corinthians 4:7-9, 16-18; and Hebrews 10:35-36. (Also keep in mind what you learned about Job's trials). What role does God play in the cause or solution of our earthly problems?

● Describe a time when you faced a challenging situation (like the ones Roy Hobbs and Job faced) and won—or at least persevered. What lessons did you learn from this experience? What new things did you learn about God?

Never Been Kissed

Trailer

How do your high school experiences shape and affect your future?

The movie comedy/romance, PG-13

Josie Gellar (Drew Barrymore) finally gets her chance to write a real news story when the head of the *Chicago Sun Times* assigns her an undercover story about the state of America's youth. Josie was a big teen nerd and still can't fit in with the cool kids.

This clip (about 3 minutes)

▶ **Start** / 0:45:05 / Josie is asleep in a chair.

⏹ **Stop** / 0:48:37 / The scene goes to black.

After being ridiculed in the school hallway for unwittingly having the word loser stamped on her forehead, Josie recalls how a popular boy in her high school class humiliated her on prom night.

Additional Clip (about 2 minutes)

▶ **Start** / 1:23:10 / "Let me tell you something. I don't care about being your stupid prom queen."

⏹ **Stop** / 1:25:45 / "Find out who you are and try not be afraid of it."

Josie saves a nerdy girl from a shower of dog food and the cool kids turn on her. She's tired of their self-important attitudes and tells them that fitting in with a popular crowd because of your outsides appearances won't matter after graduation. It's what you have on the *inside* that counts in the real world.

By the Book

Matthew 6:1-2; 23:5-7; Romans 12:2-19; Philippians 2:3-8;
Colossians 3:1-10; 1 Peter 1:14-16, 2:1; 3:8-17; 1 John 2:15-17

Where to take it

What advice would you give to a new high school freshman about surviving his or her next four years of school?

Read Romans 12:2-19; Philippians 2:3-8; Colossians 3:1-10; 1 Peter 1:14-16, 2:1, 3:8-17; and 1 John 2:15-17. List the words of advice that you find within these passages that could be applied to getting along with others at school and in extracurricular activities.

How would your classmates react or respond if you were suddenly perfect and could follow all of this advice all of the time? How would your friends react? Your teachers and principal?

If you were to choose just one area to improve—for example, filthy language (Colossians 3:8) or trying not to repay "insult with insult" (1 Peter 3:9)—which one would you choose?

If you were able to do better in your chosen area for even one week, who do you think would notice the change in you first?

Define popularity, and then describe why people value it so highly. If you believe popularity becomes less important as a person gets older, explain why this is so.

Read Matthew 6:1-2 and 23:5-7. How do these descriptions compare with today's idea of popularity? Now rewrite these verses as though they're describing the popularity contests that go on in your school.

127

Notting Hill *Trailer*

Have you told anyone about the real you?

The movie   comedy/romance/drama, PG-13

Beautiful American movie star Anna Scott (Julia Roberts) has little time for relationships and absolutely no luck with love until she meets William Thacker (Hugh Grant), a frumpy, British bookstore owner. After a false start or two, this unlikely pair begins dating in secret. But when the British press gets wind of their romance, William and Anna discover how different one person's world and perspective can be from the other's.

This clip   (just under 4 minutes)

- ▶ **Start** / 0:40:00 / "Having you here, Anna, firmly establishes what I long suspected."

- ■ **Stop** / 0:43:44 / "No, nice try, gorgeous, but you're not fooling anyone."

Anna and William attend a birthday dinner for his sister. After dessert the host suggests that guests share their sad stories with the group, and the person with the saddest one will be awarded the last brownie. One friend shares that he is paid well to do a job he doesn't understand. The birthday girl says she gets paid very little and chooses boyfriends who are bad for her. The hostess has a loving husband, but she's confined to a wheelchair and can't have a baby. This exercise illustrates that everyone experiences heartache—but we don't have to suffer through it alone.

By the Book

Proverbs 24:17; Romans 12:15-16; 2 Corinthians 10:12, 17-18;
Galatians 6:2-5; Ephesians 4:2-3; Colossians 3:9-10; 1 Peter 3:8

Where to take it

● Why would someone want to relive his sad story (beside competing for a brownie reward)?

● How do you comfort someone who's going through a hard time?

● *Everyone thinks she's a good listener, but few people really are.* Explain why you agree or disagree with this statement.

● Read Romans 12:15-16; Ephesians 4:2-3; Colossians 3:9-10; and 1 Peter 3:8. What does a good listener do during a conversation?

● List the actions of a good listener that are hard for you. Why are they difficult for you?

● List the actions of a good listener that you find easy. Explain why you don't have a problem with these.

● *When someone tells you his problems, you need to be able to offer him insight and advice.* Explain why you agree or disagree with this statement.

● When you compare yourself to someone else, what are the positive results? What are the negative results?

● Read Proverbs 24:17; 2 Corinthians 10:12, 17-18; and Galatians 6:2-5. How do you usually feel when you compare yourself to others? Describe a time when you compared yourself or your situation with someone who had it worse than you did. How did you respond?

Who's your hero?

The movie drama, PG

Homer Hickam (Jake Gyllenhaal) is a high school student in
Coalwood, West Virginia. The year is 1957—the dawn of the space
race. As the Soviet Union launches Sputnik (the first man-made
satellite), it also unwittingly launches Homer's plans for his future—a
career involving jets and rocket design. At first the townspeople,
including Homer's father John (Chris Cooper), aren't too sure about
his crazy experiments. John believes his son should work in the coal
mines with him and earn a decent living. John refuses to
acknowledge Homer's dreams, but his approval is what Homer
desires most.

This clip (about 2 minutes)

▶ **Start** / 1:32:55 / "Will you let me out?"

■ **Stop** / 1:35:00 / Mr. Hickam is lowered into
the coal mine.

Homer goes to see his dad and tells him he's decided go against
John's wishes and pursue rocket design. John knows his boy is smart,
but he worries that Homer's dreams will lead him away from home.
Homer reassures John that no matter where this journey takes him
or who he meets along the way, his dad will always be his hero.

By the Book

Psalm 37:4-9, 23-24; Proverbs 16:1-3; 19:20-21; 23:24; Isaiah 30:20-21; Ephesians 6:1-4

Where to take it

- **?** What is a hero?

- **?** Do heroes exist today? If you think so, name a few modern examples and share what makes them heroes or heroines.

- **?** Describe one of your heroes. What characteristics that you respect does your hero have?

- **?** Read Proverbs 23:24 and Ephesians 6:1-4. How do you know if your parents approve or disapprove of your decisions? How do you respond to their disapproval?

- **?** Whose approval do you desire the most? Why are his or her opinions so important to you?

- **?** Talk about a time when you chose to go your own way or do your own thing in spite of someone's disapproval. How did it feel to go against his or her wishes? How did that person respond to your choice?

- **?** Read Psalm 37:4-9, 23-24; Proverbs 16:1-3; 19:20-21; and Isaiah 30:20-21. How can you determine if God approves of your future plans?

- **?** When do you usually seek God's guidance regarding a decision? Explain why it is—or isn't—important for you to have God's approval before you do something.

One True Thing

Trailer

Are you satisfied with your life or always looking for more?

The movie   drama, R

Ellen Gulden (Renée Zellweger) leaves her hectic life as a journalist to take care of her dying mother Kate (Meryl Streep). Back in her childhood home, Ellen resents her mother's seemingly simplistic life as a housewife and doesn't enjoy the role reversal involved in caring for her mom's needs. However, Ellen's attitude starts to change as she realizes this may be the last holiday they spend together as a family.

This clip   (about 4 minutes)

▶ **Start** / 1:32:42 / Ellen walks into her mother's bedroom.

⏹ **Stop** / 1:36:55 / "It's much more peaceful."

Kate has a heart-to-heart talk with Ellen. The older woman confronts her daughter about how angry she's been acting toward her dad lately, reminding her that pretty soon he'll be all she has left. She admits knowing why Ellen is upset with her dad but warns her not to be so hard and judgmental—two qualities that could mess up her life. Kate explains how one's expectations for marriage change over the years and tells her daughter how much easier life can be when you choose to love the things you have, instead of yearning for what you think you're missing.

By the Book

Matthew 10:37-39; Luke 12:15-34; Philippians 4:12-13; 1 Timothy 6:6-12, 17-19; Hebrews 13:5

Where to take it

- What do you expect marriage to be like?

- Compared to your parents' marriage, what do you hope to do differently if you marry? What do you want to do the same?

- What are some simple things in life that people should take the time to enjoy?

- What are some interests, activities, pursuits, or other areas of your life that prevent you from slowing down and appreciating these simple things? Which of these obstacles can easily be removed?

- Read Matthew 10:37-39 and Luke 12:22-34. Using these passages, and any other verses that come to mind, describe the kind of life God wants you to live.

- Describe a time when you felt contentment. How often do you feel this way?

- Read Luke 12:15-21; Philippians 4:12-13; 1 Timothy 6:6-12, 17-19; and Hebrews 13:5. What desires, besides the desire for more money or possessions, keep a person from feeling content? Does God approve of these desires?

- Thoreau once said, "Most men lead a life of quiet desperation." What do you think he meant?

133

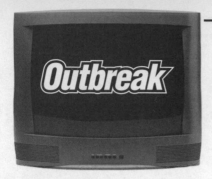

Outbreak Trailer

What addictions or temptations challenge you?

The movie action/drama/thriller, R

The deadly Motaba virus was originally part of a U.S. government experiment in 1967. Only two men know it exists, and they thought they had it safely locked away. But Motaba is back with a vengeance, killing off an entire village in Zaire. Scientists, including Sam Daniels (Dustin Hoffman), have never seen viral cells kill a person within five hours of infection before. Sam asks the Centers for Disease Control to issue a nationwide warning, but they see no reason to alarm Americans about a virus that isn't likely to leave Africa. Meanwhile an infected monkey is illegally smuggled into San Francisco. Sam and his team must work fast to find the tiny mammal, develop a vaccine, and ultimately stop the virus from destroying the population of a small town—and maybe even the nation.

This clip (just under 1 minute)

▶ **Start** / 0:41:03 / A couple walks across the street to a movie theatre.

■ **Stop** / 0:41:55 / "Water. Help me, I need water."

This scene shows a man coughing up tiny viral particles, which rapidly move through the air in a packed movie theater, landing on—and infecting—a number of people nearby.

By the Book

John 4:4-15; 7:37-39; Romans 6:20-23; 7:15-20; 13:12-14;
1 Peter 5:8

Where to take it

🅠 What are some examples of bad habits
that start small and grow into bigger
problems?

🅠 *People are unaware of the small sins in
their lives until they become bigger,
uncontrollable problems.* What is
true—and false—about this
statement?

🅠 What are some ways that seemingly
small, insignificant behaviors or
attitudes can harm people?

🅠 Read Romans 6:20-23; 7:15-20; 13:12-
14; and 1 Peter 5:8. What do these
passages tell you about sin?

🅠 In this scene the infected man begged for
some water before he collapsed. What is the living water that
the Bible talks about?

🅠 Read John 4:4-15 and 7:37-39. In what ways has God's living
water quenched your thirst?

Patch Adams

Trailer

Are you more likely to help people reach their dreams or stand in their way?

The movie   comedy/drama, PG-13

Hunter "Patch" Adams (Robin Williams) is a medical student who believes that laughter is the best medicine. Except for the hospital administrators, everyone loves his unorthodox approach of treating the patient, not the disease. Patch asks patients about their dreams, then makes them come true.

This clip   (just under 4 minutes)

▶ **Start** / 0:38:01 / "An enema bulb?"

⏹ **Stop** / 0:41:50 / "How about a poodle?"

Patch explains his approach to treating patients with compassion and humor to his classmate, Carin Fisher (Monica Potter). Then he enlists her help in carrying out the safari fantasy of a dying man, using balloon animal costumes and a toy gun.

Additional Clip   (about 4 minutes)

▶ **Start** / 1:39:22 / Interior of a courtroom.

⏹ **Stop** / 1:43:31 / "Talk to wrong numbers... talk to everyone."

Patch is accused of practicing medicine without a license and must defend himself at a hearing before the state medical board in order to graduate. Patch condemns the university for teaching doctors to distance themselves from patients. He feels death should be treated with humor and dignity and that a doctor's mission should be improving the quality of the life that remains. He challenges the board by saying, "You treat a disease—you win, you lose. You treat a *person*, I guarantee you'll win no matter what the outcome."

By the Book

Psalm 126; Proverbs 14:13; 17:22; Ecclesiastes 3:1-8, 12-13;
Luke 6:21; Romans 12:1; 1 Peter 3:8

Where to take it

- Why does laughter feel so good? What's one of your favorite laughter-filled memories?

- Read Proverbs 17:22. Explain why you agree or disagree with what this verse says.

- Read Psalm 126 and Luke 6:21. What hope do you find in these passages?

- Read Proverbs 14:13 and Ecclesiastes 3:1-8, 12-13. What do these passages have to say about the cycle of a person's life? Explain why these verses encourage or discourage you.

- Speaking personally, what is the purpose of your life on Earth? Who regularly reminds you of this fact? Describe this person and some of the life lessons you've learned from him.

- Even though he was criticized for it, Patch Adams went out of his way to make others smile. Describe a time when you were criticized for trying to do what was right.

- List some techniques for pursuing your dreams in the face of adversity and criticism.

The Patriot

Trailer

When was the last time you stood up for what you believed?

The movie action/drama/war, R

Colonel Benjamin Martin (Mel Gibson) is a South Carolina farmer with a tenacious pride in his French heritage. Benjamin fought during the French-Indian war, but he renounced violence after the death of his wife and is now content to farm and raise his eight children. In 1776, Benjamin's oldest son Gabriel (Heath Ledger) signs up to fight the British in the Revolutionary War and is captured by the enemy. Benjamin sets aside his pacifism and forms a regiment of Carolina patriots to help save his son.

This clip (just under 3 minutes)

▶ **Start** / 0:58:00 / Gabriel walks into the church as the congregation sings "Amen."

⬤ **Stop** / 1:00:52 / The scene ends on Gabriel's face.

During a memorial service, Gabriel makes an announcement to enlist men in the South Carolina militia. However King George was the one who ordered the hanging of the men being memorialized, trying to set an example to the rest of the colonists—and it worked. When Gabriel asks the men to get out of their pews and go fight for their freedom, no one responds. Disgusted by the men's hypocrisy, Annie Howard (Lisa Brenner) stands up and challenges them to act on the beliefs she's heard them speak about so strongly.

By the Book

Job 22:2-3; Psalm 119:9-16; Jeremiah 17:5-8; Ephesians 6:10-20; Colossians 4:2-6; 1 Thessalonians 1:2-10

Where to take it

? What are some personal convictions you aren't afraid to share with others? Or what would people say you believe?

? What convictions are you more hesitant to share? Explain what it is about these convictions that holds you back.

? Read Colossians 4:2-6 and 1 Thessalonians 1:2-10. In what ways do your actions support your beliefs?

? Read Jeremiah 17:5-8. Describe a time when your convictions were tested. What was the outcome?

? Read Psalm 119:9-16 and Ephesians 6:10-20. Describe a time when you knew you should have taken a stand for what you believed but you remained quiet instead. What kept you silent? How could you have ended the situation differently?

? Read Job 22:2-3 and honestly answer the questions asked in the passage.

The Perfect Storm

Trailer

Do the storms of life seem to drag you down?

The movie   adventure/drama/thriller, PG-13

Over the Atlantic Ocean in October 1991, a dying tropical hurricane came up from Bermuda and collided with a cold front from the Great Lakes. *The Perfect Storm* is based on the true story of how the *Andrea Gail* and her crew fought for their lives in the middle of this phenomenal weather pattern, which produced 100-foot waves at sea and caused extensive damage on land.

This clip   (about 2 minutes)

- ▶ **Start** / 1:50:14 / The Andrea Gail is being tossed around in thunderous waves.

- ■ **Stop** / 1:52:17 / Billy and Bob see the huge wave they must get over to reach safety.

Captain Billy Tyne (George Clooney) and crewmember Bobby Shatford (Mark Wahlberg) attempt to steer the *Andrea Gail* out of horrific waves and into safer waters. It seems like the worst has passed until clouds quickly cover the sky. In the end the boat must climb over a wave so mammoth, the men wonder if the fight for safer waters—and their lives—is futile.

By the Book

Job 36:15; Psalm 40:1-5, 11-17; Proverbs 27:17; Isaiah 30:18-21; Luke 8:22-25

Where to take it

🔋 Describe a storm in your life that seemed to rage on and on.

🔋 Where was God during this hard time in your life (described in the last question)? After you've answered, read Job 36:15; Psalm 40:1-5, 11-17; and Isaiah 30:18-21. How might you change your answer after reading these verses?

🔋 Read Luke 8:22-25. How would you respond if someone— maybe Jesus—were to ask you, "Where is your faith?" in the midst of that continual storm. What encouragement does this passage offer you?

🔋 Read Proverbs 27:17. Describe the role, if any, that other people played in helping you come out of this storm in one piece. How do you explain this verse?

🔋 Now describe a recurring storm in your life, a challenge that you just can't seem to shake (overspending, overeating, gossiping). How do you overcome it each time it resurfaces? Who do you turn to for help?

🔋 What do you need to do to get out from under this particular storm for good?

🔋 *God doesn't cause the storms to come into our lives, but God can get us through them.* Explain why you agree or disagree with each part of this statement.

Pleasantville

Trailer

How do you deal with scary emotions?

The movie   fantasy/comedy/drama, PG-13

David Wagner (Tobey Maguire) escapes the troubles that come from living with his divorced mother and overly hormonal sister Jennifer (Reese Witherspoon) by watching reruns of the 1950s hit television show *Pleasantville*. A mysterious television repairman (Don Knotts) replaces the Wagners' broken remote control. When they use the new remote, David and Jennifer find themselves transported to Pleasantville. At first David relishes in the familiar surroundings, but gradually he understands that having a pleasant but stagnant life isn't really *living* after all.

This clip   (about 4 minutes)

▶ **Start** / 1:42:17 / "Bud Parker William Johnson."

■ **Stop** / 1:46:40 / "And you can't stop something that's inside you."

At a court hearing, David is formally charged with "desecrating a public building" (with a colorful mural). However it soon becomes apparent that he's also being blamed for the growing tension between the "colorized" and the black-and-white townspeople. David claims the Technicolor crowd only *seems* different because they've chosen to discover and embrace what's deep inside them—new, but not always pleasant, feelings like silly, sexy, dangerous, and brave. He claims these emotions are inside everyone all the time, a person just has to find the courage to look for them.

By the Book

Matthew 9:16-17; 23:25-28; 25:14-29

Where to take it

- If you had a choice, which world would you choose—black-and-white (perfect and painless) or colorful (exciting but painful)? Why?

- What emotions—good or bad—do you keep inside because expressing them isn't considered proper? What are the short-term effects of stuffing your emotions instead of sharing them with someone? What are the long-term effects?

- Read Matthew 23:25-28. What is Jesus' problem with the Pharisees and teachers of the law? Talk about that.

- Can you think of a time when you've acted more clean or righteous on the outside than you've felt on the inside? If you feel comfortable doing so, talk about it. What led you to act like this? How did it affect you and your relationships? What did it take for you to realize you weren't being authentic with people?

- What's something you'd love to try but don't because fear holds you back? Explain what it would take to get you to try it.

- Read the parable of the talents in Matthew 25:14-29. Describe some of the talents you aren't using to their full potential. How could you use your gifts to help someone else?

- Read Matthew 9:16-17. What is the parallel between wineskins and becoming a Christian? What other Scripture can you find that talks about what followers of Christ should do with their old ways of living?

- In this scene David's "partner in crime," Bill, tries to make a deal with the judge, offering to use fewer colors when he paints in the future. How would this kind of compromise affect Bill's level of fulfillment? How can trying to please people affect the way you use your gifts?

143

The Prince of Egypt

Trailer

What's keeping you from being all God created you to be?

The movie
animation/family/musical/ drama, PG

Rameses (voice of Ralph Fiennes) and Moses (voice of Val Kilmer) couldn't be more different. Since birth Rameses was groomed to become the next Pharaoh. By Pharaoh's orders Moses was supposed to be thrown into the Nile. But God had other plans. In an ironic plot twist that only God could orchestrate, Pharaoh's wife found Moses floating in a basket and made him her son. While growing up in the palace, Moses frequently provoked his brother Rameses to do mischief with him, often getting the older boy in trouble with their father. When Rameses becomes the ruling Pharaoh, God asks Moses to go back to Egypt and provoke his brother again—this time to let God's people go.

This clip (5 minutes)

- **Start** / 0:42:47 / Moses notices a sheep wandering off and follows it.
- **Stop** / 0:47:47 / Moses stands beside the unharmed bush in awe.

Using a burning bush to get Moses' attention, God asks Moses to lead the Israelites to freedom in the Promised Land. At first Moses can't believe the Lord is talking to him, but once God makes his identity known, Moses struggles to believe that God wants *him* to free the Israelites. Isn't somebody else better equipped for this job?

By the Book

Exodus 3:1–4:23, 29-31; Romans 9:14-24

Where to take it

- Why do you think God used a burning bush to talk to Moses? If God wanted to get your attention quickly today, what should he use?

- What did it mean when God said, "Take the sandals from your feet, for the place on which you stand is holy ground"?

- In this clip the same actor provided the voices of Moses and God. What's significant about portraying God's voice in this way? Why not use a more distinctive voice?

- Have you ever heard the still, small voice of God? Describe how you knew God was speaking to you. Did it sound like your voice?

- At the end of this scene, God says, "You shall do my wonders. I shall be with you, Moses." What wonders have you experienced for the cause of Christ? How does God show you that he will be with you?

- In what ways, if any, are you like Moses?

- What excuses do people offer when they disobey God? Describe a time when you said no or not now to God.

- In what areas of your life do you struggle to trust God?

- Read Romans 9:14-24. What's your response to this passage about God's sovereignty? How would you explain God's sovereignty in your own words?

Trailer

What makes people run away?

The movie   comedy/romance, PG

While up against a deadline for his *USA Today* column, Ike Graham (Richard Gere) is desperate for an idea. A stranger gives him one— Maggie Carpenter (Julia Roberts), the runaway bride. Maggie earned her nickname after leaving several fiancés in the dust on their wedding days. After getting a few more details from jilted fiancé number three, Ike writes a column about Maggie's man-eating ways. Maggie responds by sending a letter of complaint to his editor and demanding that Ike's column be dropped. When Ike suddenly finds himself unemployed, he decides to find out the truth about this woman's fear of commitment and to redeem himself as a journalist.

This clip   (just under 3 minutes)

- ▶ **Start** / 1:34:00 / Maggie's bridesmaids are walking up the aisle.

- ⏹ **Stop** / 1:36:45 / A Fed Ex truck drives out of sight with Maggie aboard.

It's Maggie and Ike's wedding day. After thoroughly researching Maggie for a more accurate follow-up story, Ike believes he really knows her. He also believes *this* will be the day when Maggie stays at the altar and becomes his wife. As Maggie nervously walks down the aisle, a camera flash breaks her eye contact with Ike and she starts to have second thoughts—again.

● **commitment, reliability, faithfulness**

By the Book

Philippians 2:1-11; 2 Timothy 1:7-10; 1 John 4:18

Where to take it

- ❓ On a scale from one (you can't count on me for anything) to 10 (I always follow through on my promises), how would you rate your reliability? How would others rate you—parents, teachers, coaches, friends? Explain the reason for any significant differences between these ratings.

- ❓ What advice would you give someone who wants to be more reliable? Explain your thoughts about whether a person can learn to be more reliable.

- ❓ Why are people afraid of commitment? What kinds of commitments (besides romantic ones) can be scary?

- ❓ How does Philippians 2:1-11 apply to being committed? What do you find encouraging about this passage?

- ❓ Describe a time, including the end result, when you wanted to commit to something but were afraid. If you could live this moment over again, what would you do differently?

- ❓ Look at 2 Timothy 1:7-10 and 1 John 4:18. How do these passages apply to you? How can these verses help you make tough decisions about commitment or other areas of your life?

147

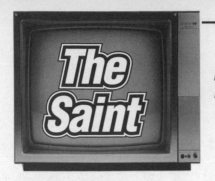

The Saint

Trailer

How important is a name?

The movie — action/romance/thriller, PG-13

Simon Templar (Val Kilmer) is a professional thief and a man of a thousand faces who uses the names of obscure saints for aliases. Simon wants to get out of the high-tech crime business, so for his final high-paying job he agrees to steal a cold fusion formula for an ambitious Russian politician. It should be the easiest job of Simon's career, until he falls in love with Dr. Emma Russell (Elisabeth Shue), the insecure Oxford scientist who holds the secret to the cold fusion phenomenon.

This clip (about 2 minutes)

▶ **Start** / 0:40:30 / "I don't even know your name."

⏹ **Stop** / 0:42:50 / Thomas Moore gets up from the table.

Emma is taken aback when Simon accurately describes her—from her determination to her love of fish—and pretends to know these things because he knows her name. (Simon actually snooped around her flat one day.) When Emma asks for a turn, Simon is torn. Professionally, he needs to stay detached, but personally he wants Emma to know the *real* Simon—a man he can no longer identify. So Simon compromises and uses his alias, Thomas Moore. Emma soon proves that she didn't need his real name (or an afternoon in his flat) to see his true character.

By the Book

Genesis 17:5-8, 15-16; 32:28-30; Psalm 139

Where to take it

2 Read Genesis 17:5-8, 15-16 and 32:28-30. What does your name mean? Is it a good fit for you?

2 Explain how you feel about your name. Do you like it? If not, what new name would you choose for yourself?

2 Were you named after someone? If so, how has that person lived his or her life?

2 People tend to associate certain personal qualities with the names of people they know who possess those traits: (Mother) Teresa with compassion, Billy (Graham) with godliness and integrity, Adolf (Hitler) with brutality. With that in mind, what reaction or response do you want your name to produce in others?

2 Emma said Simon was running from his past. What causes people to run away? Give examples of what you've run from in the past.

2 Is it possible to totally escape something from your past? If it were possible, explain why it would be healthy or unhealthy to do so.

2 Read Psalm 139. How does God feel about you? Describe your response to this psalm.

2 Emma tells Thomas: "You don't have to be afraid of who you are because you're beautiful." Describe what makes you beautiful—inside and out. (This isn't easy to do, but it's a good exercise in self-discovery. If you aren't sure how to respond, let the rest of your group help you list the ways you're beautiful.)

149

Schindler's List

Trailer

What holds the greatest value
for you?

The movie drama/war, R

Based on a true story, *Schindler's List* stars Liam Neeson as Oskar
Schindler, an arrogant German businessman who takes full
advantage of the moneymaking opportunities brought about by the
Nazis' rise to power during World War 2. Schindler owns a factory in
Poland and uses cheap Jewish laborers from the concentration
camps to keep it running. Over time Schindler develops compassion
for his workers and requests more Jews from the camps. By the time
Germany falls into Russian hands, Schindler lost his fortune but
spared 1,100 people from the gas chambers.

This clip (just under 5 minutes)
This clip is taken from the second tape.

- **Start** / 0:47:00 / Oskar Schindler walks
  onto the train tracks surrounded by 1100
  Jewish immigrants.

- **Stop** / 0:51:50 / Schindler looks through
  the car window at the people he saved.

As Schindler walks to the car, over 1,000 people are waiting to thank
him for saving their lives. However all the big-hearted businessman
can think about are the people he *couldn't* save. Oskar looks at his
clothes, car, and jewelry with new eyes. He now understands that if
he'd sold these things in order to save more lives, ultimately they
would have been worth so much more than they can ever be worth
in his possession.

By the Book

Matthew 19:17-26; 25:31-46; Luke 12:15-21

Where to take it

② Is the nature of money good, evil, or neutral? Why do you think so?

② Describe some things you value more highly than you should.

② Describe what you tend to undervalue or take for granted.

② What does the phrase *you can't take it with you* mean? How does this truth affect your life?

② Look at Luke 12:15-21. Explain what the phrase "rich toward God" means. (See Matthew 25:31-46 for some possible ideas.) Would you consider Oskar Schindler to be rich toward God? Do you have to have lots of money or possessions to be rich toward God?

② Describe your idea of the perfect life. What part does money play in it?

② Read Matthew 19:17-26. What did Jesus tell the rich young man? What does God require of wealthy people today?

② Explain why it might be hard for a rich person in the 21st century to accept the gift of salvation and become a Christian.

Simon Birch

Trailer

What kind of person does God use?

The movie · drama, PG

Joe Wenteworth (Joseph Mazzello) and Simon Birch (Ian Michael Smith) have a life-changing friendship. Simon was born with Morquio Syndrome, a genetic disorder that has left him with numerous physical problems. However his brain and his tongue are both sharp. While his parents and others consider his life to be a mistake, Simon knows God has a purpose for him.

This clip (about 5 minutes)

▶ **Start** / 0:28:05 / "Blessed is he whose transgressions are forgiven."

■ **Stop** / 0:33:23 / "You know what Simon? Thank you."

Simon stands up in church to argue with Reverend Russell (David Strathairn) about God's interest in the church bake sale. The minister politely tolerates the interruption, but when Simon later disrupts his Sunday school class, his teacher (Jan Hooks) puts him in timeout. After the rest of the class is dismissed, she berates Simon for thinking he's special enough to go to church or to be used by God. Fortunately, Joe's mom steps in and sets the teacher straight.

Additional Clip (just under 1 minute)

▶ **Start** / 0:02:09 / "Hi, Mr. Roberts."

■ **Stop** / 0:02:52 / Close-up shot of an armadillo statue next to Simon's gravestone.

Joe (Jim Carrey) explains why he'll always remember Simon.

By the Book

Acts 20:24; Romans 12:6-8; 1 Corinthians 12:4-26;
2 Corinthians 12:7-10; Ephesians 4:1-7, 29-32; 1 Peter 3:15-18

Where to take it

Based on what you saw and heard in these clips, what was Simon's purpose?

Explain why you agree—or disagree—that God has a purpose for everyone.

What are the chances that your God-given purpose will be a big deal to the rest of the world? Would you be disappointed if your God-given purpose is *not* one that is recognized by millions of people? Why?

Evaluate what Simon's teacher said to him based on 1 Corinthians 12:4-26 and Ephesians 4:1-7, 29-32.

What does it mean to be an instrument of God? How difficult is it to be God's instrument? What makes it so?

Look at Acts 20:24 and 1 Peter 3:15-18. What purpose is described in these passages? Is this your purpose?

On a scale of one (no problem!) to 10 (forget it!), rate how difficult it is to carry out this purpose. Explain your rating.

In the second clip Joe credits Simon for being the reason he believes in God. Describe someone who has been influential in teaching you about God. What did that person do? Who could *you* teach about God?

What are your gifts or talents? Describe some ways you could use these for God.

153

A Simple Plan

Trailer

Does money make your life better?

The movie   crime/thriller/drama, R

Brothers Hank (Bill Paxton) and Jacob Mitchell (Billy Bob Thornton) discover a single engine plane in the snowy Minnesota woods. Inside the snow-covered wreckage, they uncover a dead pilot and a bag containing four million dollars. They decide to take the bag and hide the money until spring. If no one asks about the money after the plane is found, then they'll split the cash. It all sounds simple enough, but the plan goes wrong.

This clip (about 1 minute)

▶ **Start** / 1:26:18 / "Hank, you know I've never even kissed a girl?"

⏹ **Stop** / 1:27:50 / Jacob walks to the house.

Jacob is telling Hank what he'd like to do with his share of the money. He doesn't want a fancy car, a mansion, or even a chance to travel the world. All Jacob wants are the simple things that other folks take for granted—a nice wife, a couple of kids, and a home (specifically the farm that used to belong to his parents). Hank doesn't know how to respond to Jacob's desires because he already has those things. Hank is living the life his brother desperately wants, but how can he help Jacob understand that it's a life money can't buy?

By the Book

Psalm 139; Ecclesiastes 5:18-20; Hebrews 13:5

Where to take it

- How much money would it take for you to be content for the rest of your life? Suppose you had that much money. What would you do with it?

- Pretend you have all the material possessions you could ever need. How will you spend your money?

- What's the downside to having lots of money?

- Read Ecclesiastes 5:18-20. Summarize the point of this Scripture in your own words. Which part is the hardest for you to accept or believe?

- Without naming names, can you think of anyone who's said something like, "If I just had a boyfriend (or girlfriend)—I would be so happy!" What does a romantic relationship add to a person's life? What personal needs are met by a boyfriend or girlfriend and for how long?

- Skim through the Psalms and jot down a list of the descriptors you find about God, his ways, and his relationship to us. After a few minutes look at your list and note any parallels you see between the effect God's presence has on our lives and the role a boyfriend or girlfriend is expected to play. How does a relationship with God compare to a relationship with a member of the opposite sex?

- Read Psalm 139. What personal needs does God meet in your life? How well does God know and understand you? How long will God be there for you?

Do you see dead people?

The movie thriller/drama/horror, PG-13

Child psychologist Dr. Malcolm Crowe (Bruce Willis) tries to help
Cole Sear (Haley Joel Osment), a six-year-old boy who sees ghosts
everywhere he goes. Malcolm tries to teach Cole to use his abilities
to help these troubled dead people, but the doctor eventually
discovers that Cole's case is way beyond his expertise.

This clip (just under 2 minutes)

▶ **Start** / 0:49:50 / "I want to tell you my
secret now."

⏹ **Stop** / 0:51:33 / Cole turns away from
Malcolm and shuts his eyes.

Cole anxiously reveals his secret to Malcolm—he can see and talk to
people who've died but still hang out on Earth for some reason. The
boy explains that the most amazing thing about these dead people
is that they don't seem to realize that their lives have ended, a point
Malcolm will later find troubling.

156

By the Book

Matthew 22:29-32; 24:36-51; Acts 26:8; Romans 8:10-11; 10:8-13;
1 Corinthians 15:35-44; 2 Timothy 1:7-10

Where to take it

- Explain whether you believe a person's spirit can wander around Earth after death.

- Cole says that most dead people don't realize they're dead because they only see what they want to see. Give some examples of how living people can act this way.

- What do you know or understand about the Second Coming of Jesus? What will happen to your body when Jesus returns to Earth?

- Read Matthew 22:29-32; Acts 26:8; Romans 8:10-11; and 1 Corinthians 15:35-44. Make a list of truths about life after death. What information in these verses surprises you?

- List some positive things about spending all your time with other Christians. What are some negative things about limiting your friendships in this way?

- Now describe the good and bad points of hanging out with only non-Christians.

- How many of your friends know you're a Christian? How many don't have a clue about your faith and spirituality? How many do you *wish* knew the truth?

- What makes it hard to talk about your faith or church with your friends? Why is it important to do so?

- Read Matthew 24:36-51; Romans 10:8-13; and 2 Timothy 1:7-10. How do these verses encourage you to talk to your nonbelieving friends about having a relationship with the Lord?

Trailer

What's the negative force in your life?

The movie — science fiction/family/action/ adventure, PG

Anakin Skywalker (Jake Lloyd) is a nine-year-old slave belonging to Watto, a crooked junk dealer on Tatooine. Anakin knows how to fix almost anything, but he has other amazing powers that cannot be learned or explained. When Jedi Master Qui-Gon (Liam Neeson) enters Watto's shop to look for spare parts for his ship, he immediately recognizes the Force residing in Anakin. Wanting to help the boy, Qui-Gon makes a bet with Watto: if Anakin wins the upcoming podrace, he gets parts for his ship and Anakin can go free. If not, Qui-Gon's ship belongs to Watto. Anakin's victory is bittersweet, as Watto refuses to free Anakin's mother so she can accompany her son on his journey to becoming a Jedi knight.

This clip (about 1 minute)

- ▶ **Start** / 1:26:26 / "A ship. A cup. A ship. A speeder."

- ■ **Stop** / 1:27:32 / "I sense much fear in you."

The Jedi Council evaluates Anakin's knowledge and abilities so they can decide whether to grant Qui-Gon permission to train the boy as an apprentice. Anakin's good performance convinces the panel that the Force is incredibly strong within the boy. However they also see his fear, which casts a cloud of uncertainty over his future.

By the Book

1 Samuel 12:24-25; Psalm 34; 90; 111:10

Where to take it

- Yoda says, "Fear is the path to the dark side." Describe how that statement can be true in everyday life. How do people react or respond when they're afraid?

- Yoda also says, "Fear leads to anger, anger leads to hate, hate leads to suffering." Describe how each of these feelings can feed into the next. Share an example of this from your life or someone else's (without naming names)?

- Read 1 Samuel 12:24-25 and Psalms 34; 90; and 111:10. What does it mean to fear the Lord? How is it different from being afraid of bugs or heights? List some examples of ways you can show your fear of the Lord.

- What's one of your biggest fears? How did you become of afraid of this? What can you do to overcome your fear?

- Some people believe this saying: *We hate that which we do not know.* What does *hate* mean? With that definition in mind, what does this saying mean?

- What Scriptures can you find that talk about hate? What do they say? What does God hate? What can people do to keep the wrong kind of hate out of their lives?

How do you say goodbye?

The movie drama/comedy, PG-13

Jackie Harrison (Susan Sarandon), a divorced mother of two, has terminal cancer. Her frequent medical appointments prevent her from caring for Anna (Jena Malone) and Ben (Liam Aiken) the way she used to. So the kids' father (Ed Harris) asks his new girlfriend Isabel (Julia Roberts) to step in and help. Unfortunately, she doesn't always do things the way Jackie would, which gives the kids plenty of ammunition to pit one woman against the other. When Jackie and Isabel finally have an honest talk, they decide to start being friends, hoping their new relationship will help make the transition from mom to stepmom a little smoother for the whole family after Jackie dies.

This clip (about 6 minutes)

▶ **Start** / 1:51:25 / "Merry Christmas, sweetie. I think this has your name on it."

■ **Stop** / 1:57:40 / Jackie holds her daughter.

On Christmas morning Jackie talks individually with her son and daughter, giving each child the special present she made to help them remember her and all their shared memories. She tries to reassure them that it's okay to miss her, but lets them know that she'll always be close by if they'll just remember to take her along.

By the Book

Genesis 49:1–50:14; Ecclesiastes 7:1-4

Where to take it

? If you've ever lost someone close to you, describe what people did or said that gave you comfort or peace. What words or actions made you feel worse instead of better?

? Take a look at Genesis 49:1-28. This section of Scripture describes how Jacob gave a final blessing to each of his twelve sons. Which blessing sounds the best to you? Which blessing sounds more like a curse?

? If you knew that what your parents said would come true, what final blessing would you like to receive from them?

? Now look at Genesis 49:29–50:14. Have you ever talked with your parents about what will happen after they die? Have you ever discussed matters like how you'll feel when they're gone, what they want included in their funeral, where they want to be buried, and so on? How helpful would it be for you to have this conversation with them?

? Jackie told Ben that, after she dies, the two of them can meet in their dreams. She also said, "You won't hear my voice, but deep inside you'll know what I'm saying." How might these ideas comfort a grieving child? How can these things happen after a person dies?

? *God brings death and tragedy into our lives to teach us lessons.* Explain why you agree or disagree with this statement.

? Read Ecclesiastes 7:1-4. What do these verses mean? What is your response?

The Story of Us

Trailer

Is marriage really for better or worse?

The movie comedy/romance/drama, R

Ben and Katie Jordan (Bruce Willis and Michelle Pfeiffer) have been married for 15 years. On the outside they appear to have the perfect life: two great kids, a nice home, good jobs, and close friends. Yet the only spark left between them are the ones that fly when they fight. So while the kids are off at summer camp, Ben and Katie wrestle with the question of whether to end their marriage.

This clip (just under 4 minutes)

▶ **Start** / 1:26:42 / "I think we should go to Chow Funs"

■ **Stop** / 1:30:00 / "I love you, too."

The kids are back from camp, but they don't know about their parents' decision to divorce. Ben and Katie already decided not to tell them at Chow Funs, the kids' favorite restaurant, so they plan to tell them at home instead. Now Katie changes her mind about everything—Ben, the divorce, and especially where they should go next. When she says she wants to go to Chow Funs, Ben suspects the marriage isn't over. But before he can disagree with her, Katie launches into a fast-paced explanation for why they should stay together.

By the Book

Romans 13:8-10; Ephesians 4:26, 29–5:2; James 1:19-20

Where to take it

- How does Katie's monologue strike you—too lofty, too desperate, too reasonable? What else do you notice about it?

- What things can irritate you about another person, things that you couldn't overlook in a long-term relationship?

- What things about *you* might irritate someone else? Would you be willing or able to change these things for another person?

- What are you looking for in a future spouse? Is a marriage more likely to last if the husband and wife are more alike or different? Why do you think so?

- Why do couples divorce? Which of these reasons are acceptable to God? Which are acceptable to you?

- What would you like your marriage to be like?

- What makes a great marriage? What ingredients for a lasting relationship are mentioned in the Bible? (See Romans 13:8-10; Ephesians 4:26, 29-5:2; James 1:19-20; and any others you can think of that relate to husbands and wives.)

- Describe the changes that take place in a relationship, beginning with the wedding day and continuing along a timeline of five, 15, 25, and 50 years. Over time how do the husband and wife change, both individually and as they relate to each other?

- Using the same timeline, what life events and milestones usually occur between each of these points? How would these changes affect the health of the relationship and the couple's satisfaction overall? (Think of couples you know who've been together for these periods of time, and use them as a guide for your responses.)

Toy Story 2

Trailer

Is anything worth the consequences you pay for stealing?

The movie

animation/family/comedy/ fantasy, G

Woody (voice of Tom Hanks) doesn't know he's become a rare and valuable collector's item. However, Al (voice of Wayne Knight)—an avid toy collector and owner of Al's Toy Barn—is well aware of the cowboy doll's worth and steals him to complete his Woody the Cowboy set. With an eager buyer waiting in Japan, Al intends to get very rich from this deal. Meanwhile, Buzz Lightyear (voice of Tim Allen) and the gang are on Al's trail. They have to figure out a way to rescue Woody before he gets shipped to a Tokyo museum.

This clip (about 2 minutes)

▶ **Start** / 0:15:02 / "Woody, I'm slipping."

⏹ **Stop** / 0:17:23 / "Why would someone steal Woody?"

Woody accidentally falls out the window into the family's yard sale where Al spots him. When Andy's mom refuses to sell Woody, Al steals the cowboy doll. Buzz and the gang witness the whole thing from Andy's room window, but they're too late to help.

Where to take it

Exodus 20:1-17; Deuteronomy 5:6-22; Matthew 6:19-21, 24; Luke 16:1-13; Ephesians 4:28

By the Book

❓ Without using your Bible, list the Ten Commandments. Now look at the Ten Commandments listed in Deuteronomy 5:6-22 and Exodus 20:1-17. Which ones did you forget? Which are easiest for you to keep? Which are hardest?

❓ Are the Ten Commandments listed in any particular order, like most important to least important, or are they all equally important to God? Why do you think so?

❓ Why do people steal? Read Ephesians 4:28. What reason for stealing is implied in this verse? What's the connection between boredom and misbehavior?

❓ Are there circumstances under which you consider stealing to be acceptable? Talk about that.

❓ Read Luke 16:1-13. What is your response to the manager's actions? What was his motivation for cutting those debts in half?

❓ Look at Luke 16:9. What does it mean?

❓ There's a bumper sticker that says, "He who dies with the most toys wins!" Describe how people's lives are affected by that attitude.

❓ Look at Matthew 6:19-21. How does this passage cause you to reevaluate your perspective on owning things? How does a person "store up...treasures in heaven"?

❓ What nonmaterial things do people steal from each other?

❓ Which hurts more—losing something material (like money, a leather jacket, a CD) or something intangible (like the things you listed in the previous question)? Explain the reasons for your choice.

U-571

Trailer

What makes a great leader?

The movie action/drama/thriller/war, PG-13

World War 2 American reconnaissance agents discover that an Enigma—a special communications coding device—is aboard a sinking German submarine. This could be an invaluable tool for the Allies, so the United States Navy sends a submarine crew to capture it. Once the special team boards the sub and locates the machine, their ship and crewmates are blown out of the water. Now they must figure out how to keep the enemy sub afloat so they can escape to safer waters and deliver the Enigma into Allied hands.

This clip (about 2 minutes)

▶ **Start** / 0:30:18 / "I know the men like you."

◼ **Stop** / 0:32:20 / Lt. Tyler walks away after watching a crewmember write a letter.

Lt. Andrew Tyler (Matthew McConaughey) asks his lieutenant commander why he was denied a promotion. Mike (Bill Paxton) describes how Andrew's big-brother rapport with the crew makes him a good shipmate but an ineffective submarine captain. He goes on to say that emotions can't overrule wisdom during a crisis. A leader must be willing to lay the lives of his crew on the line—and live with the consequences. At this moment Andrew has a vague inkling of the demands of leadership, but they will become abundantly clear to him within a matter of hours.

By the Book

Joshua 1:6-9; 2 Chronicles 1:7-12; Romans 12:6-8; Hebrews 13:7;
1 Peter 5:1-4

Where to take it

- In this scene Mike says a submarine captain can't hesitate—he must act. When you make decisions in the middle of a crisis, is it better to go with your gut instincts or carefully consider your options? What have been the results when you've taken either of these approaches?

- Read Joshua 1:6-9; 2 Chronicles 1:7-12; Romans 12:6-8; and 1 Peter 5:1-4. Make a list of the leadership qualities mentioned in these passages.

- Describe Jesus as a leader.

- Read Hebrews 13:7. Name a great leader. (It doesn't have to be a Christian leader.) What are some of the qualities that make—or made— this person great?

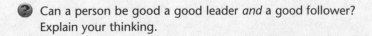

- Compare being a follower with being a leader.

- Can a person be good a good leader *and* a good follower? Explain your thinking.

- Romans 12:6-8 refers to leadership as a gift from God. Is this one of your gifts? If so, what aspects of leading do you enjoy the most? Which parts of leadership could you live without?

What about Bob?

Trailer

How merciful are you?

The movie — comedy, PG

Bob Wiley (Bill Murray) is a neurotic psychiatric patient who follows his psychiatrist on vacation. Dr. Leo Marvin (Richard Dreyfuss) is irritated by Bob's stalking behavior; however, Leo's family takes a liking to Bob and wants him to stay. Out of complete frustration, Leo makes a number of desperate attempts to get Bob to leave them alone.

This clip (about 1 minute)

▶ **Start** / 0:52:15 / "Your book is going to do a lot of good for a lot of people."

⏹ **Stop** / 0:53:37 / "I just never gave up hope."

Bob tries to rescue Leo who's choking on a chicken bone. Apparently unschooled in the ways of the Heimlich maneuver, Bob throws Leo on the couch and starts jumping up and down on his back until the bone flies free. Bob's painful attempt to help Leo gives the doctor one more reason to try to kick Bob out of their summer home.

By the Book

Matthew 18:21-35; Luke 6:27-36; Ephesians 2:1-10;
Colossians 3:12-14; James 2:14-16; 1 Peter 3:8-9

Where to take it

● Without naming names, describe some people who are difficult to love. What makes them so unlovable?

● Now describe the things that make *you* unlovable to other people.

● How would you characterize your attitude toward the unlovable? Why do you feel this way about them?

● Read Matthew 18:21-35. How do your relationships with the unlovable people and with God compare with the characters in this parable?

● What's so great about God's mercy toward you? (Look up Ephesians 2:1-10 to jog your memory.)

● What are some ways to improve an unmerciful attitude? (Look at Colossians 3:12-14 and 1 Peter 3:8-9 for ideas.) How does mercy help someone let go of past hurts and pain?

● What makes it difficult for a person to step out of her comfort zone and help others?

● Read Luke 6:27-36 and James 2:14-16. How can you translate these passages into real-life actions?

● List some practical ways that you can step out of your comfort zone this week and serve others.

Where the Heart Is

Trailer

How have lies affected your life?

The movie — comedy/drama, PG-13

Abandoned at age five by her mother, Novalee Nation (Natalie Portman) is now 17, pregnant, and on her way to the west coast with her boyfriend Willy Jack Pickens (Dylan Bruno). While she's inside Wal-Mart to take a bathroom break, he takes off and leaves her stranded. Novalee is alone and desperate, so she secretly moves into the discount store until her baby girl is born. Afterward the unexpected generosity of the townspeople, who accept them without hesitation, teaches Novalee that she does have great worth and deserves to have a better life.

This clip — (about 1 minute)

- ▶ **Start** / 1:48:18 / "I came back to tell you something."

- ■ **Stop** / 1:49:37 / "Yeah, I do."

Novalee meets up with Willy Jack after he loses his legs in an accident. He expresses regret over the way he treated Novalee, and then he admits he's told so many lies over the years he's forgotten the truth. She asks him why he lied to her, and Willy says, "Why does anyone lie? Because they're scared or crazy or just mean...there's a million reasons to lie." His honest response convicts Novalee about a lie she just told the man that she loves.

By the Book

Proverbs 21:23; Matthew 12:36-37; Acts 5:1-11

Where to take it

2️⃣ Willy Jack suggests that people lie out of fear. Explain why you agree or disagree.

2️⃣ Willy Jack also said, "Sometimes you tell a lie so big, it changed your whole life." How can lies change someone's whole life? If it's true for you, describe a time when a lie changed your life.

2️⃣ Read Acts 5:1-11 about Ananias and Saphhira. What was the consequence of their lies? How did their deaths affect the church? Do you think something like this could happen today?

2️⃣ What are some other—nonfatal—consequences of lying?

2️⃣ What are some eternal consequences? (See Matthew 12:36-37.)

2️⃣ Is it possible for a person to be completely honest all the time? Why or why not?

While You Were Sleeping

Trailer

Have you ever secretly been in love?

The movie comedy/family/romance, PG

Lucy Moderatz (Sandra Bullock), a Chicago Transit Authority worker, is attracted to a handsome commuter, Peter Callaghan (Peter Gallagher). He comes through her station every day but never notices her. When Peter is robbed and knocked unconscious onto the tracks, Lucy acts quickly to save his life. Now Peter is in a coma, and, thanks to a nurse's misunderstanding, his family believes that Lucy is the fiancée they've never met. They're so excited to be involved in Peter's life again, Lucy doesn't want to hurt them with the truth. She really enjoys being a part of their family, but she knows that the longer she pretends, the trickier life will become— especially once Peter wakes up.

This clip (just under 3 minutes)

▶ **Start** / 0:17:10 / Lucy walks into the hospital.

⏹ **Stop** / 0:20:00 / Lucy is sitting next to Peter's hospital bed.

Unable to sleep after the excitement of the day, Lucy returns to the hospital in the middle of the night to sit by Peter's bedside. Lucy pours out her heart, telling Peter a little bit about her life, how she fell in love with him at first sight, and the ups and downs of living alone.

By the Book

Ruth 1-4; Psalm 68:4-6; Proverbs 13:12; Matthew 14:22-23;
Luke 5:12-16

Where to take it

- Why is it hard to tell people how we feel about them?

- When do you tend to learn more about life, yourself, or God—
  when things are going well or not so great? Why is that the case?

- Read Proverbs 13:12. What does this verse mean? How does it
  relate to this discussion?

- What's the longest you've waited for something (this could be a
  possession, a relationship, or anything else you really wanted)?
  Explain how you felt when it was finally yours. Was it worth the
  wait? Would you have felt the same if you'd gotten it instantly?

- Summarize the story of Naomi from the book of Ruth. How
  might God have eased Naomi's loneliness after her husband and
  sons died? (See Psalm 68:4-6.) How long did she have to wait?

- How would you describe Ruth? What characteristics did she
  have that were a blessing to Naomi?

- Describe someone in your life with qualities like Ruth's. How
  have they been a blessing to you?

- Read Matthew 14:22-23 and Luke 5:12-16. Why did Jesus need
  to get away from it all? What steps are necessary for you to get
  away and talk to God on a more regular basis?

RESOURCES FROM YOUTH SPECIALTIES

Ideas Library

Ideas Library on CD-ROM 2.0
Administration, Publicity, & Fundraising
Camps, Retreats, Missions, & Service Ideas
Creative Meetings, Bible Lessons, & Worship Ideas
Crowd Breakers & Mixers
Discussion & Lesson Starters
Discussion & Lesson Starters 2
Drama, Skits, & Sketches
Drama, Skits, & Sketches 2
Drama, Skits, & Sketches 3
Games
Games 2
Games 3
Holiday Ideas
Special Events

Bible Curricula

Creative Bible Lessons from the Old Testament
Creative Bible Lessons in 1 & 2 Corinthians
Creative Bible Lessons in Galatians and Philippians
Creative Bible Lessons in John
Creative Bible Lessons in Romans
Creative Bible Lessons on the Life of Christ
Creative Bible Lessons in Psalms
Downloading the Bible Kit
Wild Truth Bible Lessons
Wild Truth Bible Lessons 2
Wild Truth Bible Lessons—Pictures of God
Wild Truth Bible Lessons—Pictures of God 2

Topical Curricula

Creative Junior High Programs from A to Z, Vol. 1 (A-M)
Creative Junior High Programs from A to Z, Vol. 2 (N-Z)
Girls: 10 Gutsy, God-Centered Sessions on Issues That Matter to Girls
Guys: 10 Fearless, Faith-Focused Sessions on Issues That Matter to Guys
Good Sex
Live the Life! Student Evangelism Training Kit

The Next Level Youth Leader's Kit
Roaring Lambs
So What Am I Gonna Do with My Life?
Student Leadership Training Manual
Student Underground
Talking the Walk
What Would Jesus Do? Youth Leader's Kit
Wild Truth Bible Lessons
Wild Truth Bible Lessons 2
Wild Truth Bible Lessons—Pictures of God
Wild Truth Bible Lessons—Pictures of God 2

Discussion Starters

Discussion & Lesson Starters (Ideas Library)
Discussion & Lesson Starters 2 (Ideas Library)
EdgeTV
Every Picture Tells a Story
Get 'Em Talking
Keep 'Em Talking!
High School TalkSheets—Updated!
More High School TalkSheets—Updated!
High School TalkSheets from Psalms and Proverbs—Updated!
Junior High-Middle School TalkSheets—Updated!
More Junior High-Middle School TalkSheets—Updated!
Junior High-Middle School TalkSheets from Psalms and Proverbs—Updated!
Real Kids: Short Cuts
Real Kids: The Real Deal—on Friendship, Loneliness, Racism, & Suicide
Real Kids: The Real Deal—on Sexual Choices, Family Matters, & Loss
Real Kids: The Real Deal—on Stressing Out, Addictive Behavior, Great Comebacks, & Violence
Real Kids: Word on the Street
Small Group Qs
Have You Ever...?
Unfinished Sentences
What If...?
Would You Rather...?

Drama Resources

Drama, Skits, & Sketches (Ideas Library)
Drama, Skits, & Sketches 2 (Ideas Library)
Drama, Skits, & Sketches 3 (Ideas Library)
Dramatic Pauses
Spontaneous Melodramas
Spontaneous Melodramas 2
Super Sketches for Youth Ministry

Game Resources

Games (Ideas Library)
Games 2 (Ideas Library)
Games 3 (Ideas Library)
Junior High Game Nights
More Junior High Game Nights
Play It!
Screen Play CD-ROM

Additional Programming Resources

(also see Discussion Starters)
Camps, Retreats, Missions, & Service Ideas (Ideas Library)
Creative Meetings, Bible Lessons, & Worship Ideas (Ideas Library)
Crowd Breakers & Mixers (Ideas Library)
Everyday Object Lessons
Great Fundraising Ideas for Youth Groups
More Great Fundraising Ideas for Youth Groups
Great Retreats for Youth Groups
Great Talk Outlines for Youth Ministry
Holiday Ideas (Ideas Library)
Incredible Questionnaires for Youth Ministry
Kickstarters
Memory Makers
Special Events (Ideas Library)
Videos That Teach
Videos That Teach 2
Worship Services for Youth Groups

Quick Question Books

Have You Ever...?
Small Group Qs
Unfinished Sentences
What If...?
Would You Rather...?

Videos & Video Curricula

Dynamic Communicators Workshop
EdgeTV
Live the Life! Student Evangelism Training Kit
Make 'Em Laugh!
Purpose-Driven™ Youth Ministry Training Kit
Real Kids: Short Cuts
Real Kids: The Real Deal—on Friendship, Loneliness, Racism, & Suicide
Real Kids: The Real Deal—on Sexual Choices, Family Matters, & Loss
Real Kids: The Real Deal—on Stressing Out, Addictive Behavior, Great Comebacks, & Violence
Real Kids: Word on the Street
Student Underground
Understanding Your Teenager Video Curriculum
Youth Ministry Outside the Lines

Especially for Junior High

Creative Junior High Programs from A to Z, Vol. 1 (A-M)
Creative Junior High Programs from A to Z, Vol. 2 (N-Z)
Junior High Game Nights
More Junior High Game Nights
Junior High-Middle School TalkSheets—Updated!
More Junior High-Middle School TalkSheets—Updated!
Junior High-Middle School TalkSheets from Psalms and Proverbs—Updated!
Wild Truth Journal for Junior Highers
Wild Truth Bible Lessons
Wild Truth Bible Lessons 2
Wild Truth Journal—Pictures of God
Wild Truth Bible Lessons—Pictures of God
Wild Truth Bible Lessons—Pictures of God 2

Student Resources

Downloading the Bible: A Rough Guide to the New Testament

Downloading the Bible: A Rough Guide to the Old Testament

Grow for It! Journal through the Scriptures

So What Am I Gonna Do with My Life?

Spiritual Challenge Journal: The Next Level

Teen Devotional Bible

What (Almost) Nobody Will Tell You about Sex

What Would Jesus Do? Spiritual Challenge Journal

Clip Art

Youth Group Activities (print)

Clip Art Library Version 2.0 (CD-ROM)

Digital Resources

Clip Art Library Version 2.0 (CD-ROM)

Great Talk Outlines for Youth Ministry

Hot Illustrations CD-ROM

Ideas Library on CD-ROM 2.0

Screen Play CD-ROM

Youth Ministry Management Tools

Professional Resources

Administration, Publicity, & Fundraising (Ideas Library)

Dynamic Communicators Workshop

Great Talk Outlines for Youth Ministry

Help! I'm a Junior High Youth Worker!

Help! I'm a Small-Group Leader!

Help! I'm a Sunday School Teacher!

Help! I'm an Urban Youth Worker!

Help! I'm a Volunteer Youth Worker!

Hot Illustrations for Youth Talks

More Hot Illustrations for Youth Talks

Still More Hot Illustrations for Youth Talks

Hot Illustrations for Youth Talks 4

How to Expand Your Youth Ministry

How to Speak to Youth...and Keep Them Awake at the Same Time

Junior High Ministry (Updated & Expanded)

Make 'Em Laugh!

The Ministry of Nurture

Postmodern Youth Ministry

Purpose-Driven™ Youth Ministry

Purpose-Driven™ Youth Ministry Training Kit

So That's Why I Keep Doing This!

Teaching the Bible Creatively

A Youth Ministry Crash Course

Youth Ministry Management Tools

The Youth Worker's Handbook to Family Ministry

Academic Resources

Four Views of Youth Ministry & the Church

Starting Right

Youth Ministry That Transforms